Abram Child Dayton

Last Days of Knickerbocker Life in New York

Abram Child Dayton

Last Days of Knickerbocker Life in New York

ISBN/EAN: 9783337111359

Printed in Europe, USA, Canada, Australia, Japan

Cover: Foto ©ninafisch / pixelio.de

More available books at **www.hansebooks.com**

OF

KNICKERBOCKER LIFE

IN

NEW YORK.

BY

ABRAM C. DAYTON.

NEW YORK:
GEORGE W. HARLAN, PUBLISHER,
19 PARK PLACE.

1882.

INTRODUCTORY.

A decade has well nigh passed since the following pages were penned. They will be perused now with added interest, for their author bade farewell to earth in August, 1877, and is sleeping by his father's side in Greenwood. The last few years of his life were spent in retirement. His impaired health of body found relaxation in intellectual employment, and many will remember how inexhaustible was the fund of anecdote and pleasant humor, with which he was wont to entertain the household circle, concerning "New York forty years ago."

It would seem as though these talks of other days awakened congenial memories, for when he died, there was discovered a neatly rolled manuscript—now unfolded to the public, letter for letter and line for line, just as he wrote and left it. He was witness to the scenes described, and contemporary with the events detailed. Such of his "troops of friends" whose eyes may meet these pictures of the past, will recall the courtly manner, the amiable, sparkling flow of cultured conversation, the graceful modesty and unreserved honesty which charmed, attracted and won all who came within his environment. Of him may be said, in the words of the master limner of human characteristics:

> "A sweeter and a lovelier gentleman,
> Framed in the prodigality of nature;
> *   *   *   *   *
> The spacious world cannot again afford."

C. W. D.

New York, June, 1880.

PREFACE.

If it be an admitted fact that "a man is known by the company he keeps," it cannot be a wrong proposition, that a state of society can best be described and understood by a "bird's-eye view" of habits, customs, occupations and amusements which ruled in every day life at that particular epoch. In the endeavor to present these peculiarities, it matters little if occasional discrepancies, or even exaggerations should creep into details, which are honestly intended to be truthful and, in the main, exact. Time, despite the most conscientious resolves, will light up pleasurable reminiscences of the past with an enhanced glow; it also will throw a denser shadow over recollections of those dark spots met with even in the sunny stage of childhood. Due allowance should always be made for the irresistible influence of prejudice; once engendered it never slumbers; it grows with our growth, strengthens with our strength, and as if it had become a dominant part of our being, rules supreme over man's warring powers, when age weakens reason. The impressions made by early associations are indelibly stamped—

——; " for lives there one
Whose infant breath was drawn, or boyhood's days
Of happiness were passed beneath that sun,
That in his manhood's prime can calmly gaze
Upon that bay, or on that mountain stand,
Nor feel the prouder of his native land."

PREFACE.

The landmarks of the Knickerbocker era are one by one disappearing, and very soon all will be swept from the face of Manhattan Island; and scarcely a vestige remains to bring to mind the staid customs and primitive mode of life which ruled in New York only forty years ago.

Forty years ago New York was by comparison a village; one cargo of the mammoth Great Eastern would have stocked its warehouses with luxuries; the passengers of one train of cars from the far West would have overflowed its houses of entertainment; its limited places of amusement were kept alive, but the managers did not amass wealth; its quiet streets offered little inducement for display, but at the same time they afforded limited scope for detective skill; its aggregate municipal outlay would scarcely be considered an object by a modern politician. Home with its legitimate influences ruled supreme, and to the unintroduced traveler from the old world our city offered but few attractions. It was unhesitatingly pronounced *dull* by the English sporting gentleman, "*horrible*" by the Parisian who had revelled in the ever changing pleasures of the gay Capital.

After New York emerged from the financial crash of 1837, occasioned primarily by the disastrous conflagration of 1835, but augmented by the explosion of a land speculation which would be unheeded now, it sprang as if by magic into metropolitan proportions. It became the moneyed centre of the continent; its banks were the depositories of the almost worthless tokens with which the country was flooded during the suspension of specie payments. This sudden accumulation of doubtful securities encouraged increased individual expenditure ; rents advanced, luxuries were introduced by foreign capitalists, and the proceeds invested in the rapidly appreciating lands lying adjacent to the city limits. The now crowning "*mortgage*," to which the prudent Knickerbocker only had recourse in the last extremity, was not considered a disgraceful fixture on the family mansion, and pretentious dwellings were erected on the surroundings of Washington Parade Ground. Albion, St. Marks, Lafayette, Waverly, Washington and other grand places were inaugurated through the instrumentality of "*wild cat*" tenders, and grandfather's simple Knickerbocker home was abandoned for more sumptuous residences in fashionable quarters. This new order of things necessitated new appliances of every sort, and the *régime* of the past was banished as if by a wave of the "enchanters magic wand." History scarcely presents the parallel of this sudden, marked transition from Dutch Gotham, with its noiseless, steady routine, to metropolitan New York, with its bustling, flighty excitement.

ABRAM C. DAYTON.

New York, December, 1871.

CHAPTER FIRST.

" Human portraits faithfully drawn, are of all pictures the welcomest on human walls."   CARLYLE.

The New York of forty years ago was very unlike the New York of to-day. Its unprecedented change, or rather growth, was unheeded, and is yet not fully realized by very many of that lucky class, who, though native born, have floated along without noting passing events, contenting themselves with the enjoyment of the rich fruits borne on their ancestral *farms*. Knickerbocker frugality was a blessing to such of the present generation who can trace their genealogy on Manhattan Island for a century, while those whose titles date back only fifty years, possess millions of substantial reasons to be thankful. They have not toiled, neither have they spun; yet while they have slumbered in idle comfort, their inherited acres have changed to city lots, and city lots, no matter how situated, represent dollars and produce income.

Forty years ago Prince Street was on the very verge of civilization. Niblo's Garden was a garden in very truth, a rural spot; and it was probably leased at a rental which would now be refused for the humblest plot on the Island, though Niblo's was situated on the only thoroughfare, except the Bowery, which the city of Gotham could boast. Thousands of the occupants of brown stone mansions which grace our leading avenues are, as is well known, not "*to the manor born*." They came from the North, South, East and West when the spirit of speculation settled upon the heretofore sleeping Dutch city. As a rule they brought little with them, save the spirit of enterprise, an indomitable will, and a firm determination to win both name and fortune. The wiry, energetic sons of New Hampshire, Maine and Vermont were among the first to step to the front in the new El Dorado, and the footprints of their industrious toil are to-day plainly discernible on Manhattan Island. Previous to the advent of this adventurous horde, Gotham under its primitive rule was satisfied to leave "well enough alone," and it is through that Gotham the writer purposes to ramble with his readers, to narrate nothing but facts, to describe person, custom and locality as they existed in his youth. This ramble will not prove dry or uninstructive as the details appear on our tramp from the old Battery. The marvellous progress which a few short years have witnessed cannot fail to excite both wonder and interest as the marked changes are one by one noted.

The vast majority of the citizens of New York now consider Sunday as a day set apart for pleasure and recreation, and in that respect our city is not very far behind the gayest capitals of the old world. It is true there still lingers in our midst a slight sprinkling of the old leaven of *strict observance*, which essays to make itself seen, felt, understood, and bravely tries to do battle for the .

"*ancien régime*" against the marked and powerful encroachments of unchecked revelry. It is still decreed by Fashion that to attend church is respectable, but then the imperious dame designates where and how her votaries shall figure in the sanctuary. Matins, however, are the mode, afternoon services in the churches as a rule are unattended, and the officiating clergymen could almost with impunity repeat their morning discourses, for empty pews are not supposed to be critical hearers. The popular theory, modern to us, that Sunday was intended as a day especially set apart for out door exercise for the toiling artizan and his housed family, has been appropriated by the leaders of society, as is amply demonstrated by the fact that on no afternoon of the week is the Central Park or the Drive more crowded with equipages or more gorgeous in display of toilets and appointments. Our theaters as yet have not opened their doors on Sunday night, still the initiative step has been taken in that direction. Concert halls and gardens are in full blast during the Summer months, where bands of pretentious excellence discourse choice selections of music, styled for appearances, sacred melodies, some of which, to the unprofessional hearer, sound amazingly as if stolen from the "*Grand Duchesse*," or "*Il Nozzé*," In this rapid age some sacred stanzas may have been composed for special adaptation to the popular "*Music Lesson*," or "*Le Sabre de Mon Père*," they must have been, or such a thoroughly educated musician as Theodore Thomas would not have directed his unrivalled orchestra to intone them on Sunday night for the edification of his enrapt audience. What a contrast presents itself between the short rollicking Sunday of 1871 with its music and dance; its brilliantly lighted saloons filled with an eager crowd of pleasure seekers; its endless train of gay promenaders; its open shops in the full tide of successful traffic, and the solemn, long Knickerbocker Sabbath, when the fourth commandment was in full force. The old time Knickerbocker Sabbath was in very truth a day especially set apart for worship. The laws of society so decreed, and public opinion was a stern master then, so woe betide the man, woman or child who dared to disobey or disregard its stringent rules. From early dawn all secular affairs were religiously abstained from, the family meals were but cold collations of Saturday baked meats—it was decreed that man servant and maid servant should rest. No sound save the tolling of the church-bell broke the awful stillness. At stated hours, three times during the day, at ten o'clock, at three o'clock and at seven o'clock, stereotype processions of staid men and women, accompanied by subdued, silent children even of the most tender age slowly wended their way to church soberly and solemnly as if they were assisting at the funeral of a dear departed friend—a bare cold nod of recognition was all that was vouchsafed to the most intimate passing acquaintance. The coy maiden looked as demure as her spectacled grandmother, who led her protectingly by the hand; the youth clad in best Sunday *roundabout*, appeared as stolid as the well fed museum anaconda, for the boy had been crammed that morning with catechism, pater and mater familias bore upon their countenances the consciousness of their awful responsibility, while Betty, the help, arrayed in the brightest calico, cleanest pinafore and gayest bandanna turban trudged along in the rear of the family circle as an evidence that the family was doing its whole duty. When the bell ceased tolling and the service was about to commence, heavy iron chains were drawn tightly across the streets adjacent to the different places of worship, that no possible noise might distract the congregation in their serious meditations. This precaution seemed in a great measure to be superfluous, for the doctor's gig on its errand of mercy, or the carriage of some aged christian too infirm to walk were the only admitted departures, as beasts were also included in the Sunday code. Now and then a sly sinner or two would *harness up* for a drive on the road, and enjoy a little sweet, unlawful frolic; but such were far too cunning to select the thoroughfare but would take some unfrequented road, certain that if detected in their sinful departure, in addition to the inevitable severe reprimand for their ungodly practices, they would during an indefinite period be the prominent subjects of intercession at evening prayers.

CHAPTER SECOND.

But to the service. It was no light affair with any denomination; at the Dutch Reformed Church it was, to say the least, fearfully lugubrious and protractive. The long spun out extemporary prayers doubtless were magnificent expositions of unadulterated faith to the full grown believer, but to the youthful listener they might as well have been uttered in *Sanscrit*, the only intelligible portions being "benighted heathen," "the lake which burns with fire and brimstone," "whited sepulchres" and other kindred expressions which are uttered in truthfulness, *that we are not as other men are.* The singing was unquestionably praise, it certainly was not music. There was no instrumental accompaniment to prescribe either tune or modulation, so that free scope was both given and taken by the human voice divine, and the brother or sister who shrieked the loudest and dwelt the longest was considered the furthest advanced on the heavenly way.

The sermon was of course the crowning feature. The dominies of the time were no niggards in their appropriation of "Holy Writ," but took whole chapters, and long ones at that, for their texts. This prudent mode of procedure gave them ample scope for their denunciations of all classes and conditions of men who by reason of education had imbibed different views of the paramount duties of poor, weak, erring humanity. As there was no hour-glass on the pulpit or warning clock displayed in the bleak square edifice, the officiating dominie, merely for form's sake, consulted his ponderous gold "bull's eye," and placed it out at arm's reach before beginning his discourse, but the worthy earnest *"fisher after souls,"* with all his precautions as to time, was only restrained in his zealous labor of love by utter physical exhaustion. Men were strong then, ministers had not become affected with the bronchial disorders so prevalent in the pulpit in these latter days; their sermons were long, loud, ponderous, nay, even muscular—they clinched each telling point with a heavy right-hand blow on the sacred volume before them, as if resolved to fix it there for all coming generations. After the pewter plate had gone its accustomed round, and garnered in its pennies—a plateful of those good sized tokens was a mighty affair—another eight stanza hymn, closing with the doxology, was vehemently shouted, when followed the concluding benediction, which to-day would be considered a prayer of reasonable duration; but it was always a blessing to us youngsters, for during its delivery we were permitted to stand, while during the other portions of the exercises the custom required us to sit bolt upright, with our eyes fixed upon the pulpit with no outward show of weariness. On our sober walk home, the entertainment was limited to listening to the family comments on the doctor's discourse. Grandmother said it was full of *refreshing consolations*, father spoke of its vital power, mother thought the doctor had never been happier, while Betty and us children did not express any opinion, not merely because we were not asked, but because we were so delighted when the massive Bible was shut with a slam, which we knew hid the doctor's notes from view, and denoted a speedy termination of the sermon. The prominent points of the morning lesson were again set before us in the lengthened grace, ere we were permitted to attack the cold collation and apple pie which Betty had prepared the day before merely as a sustainer of nature, that we might be fortified in the inner man to endure the afternoon and evening services, which were nearly equal in extent and power to the grand trial of the morning.

The Knickerbocker Sabbath has lived out its generation, and doubtless accomplished the ends for which it was instituted. It was a day of rest for all save the dominie and his youthful disciples. To the former, its arduous duties must have proved fearfully wearing, even though a man of iron constitution unimpaired by luxurious living. To the latter, the seventh day was dreaded on account of its wearisome, unnatural restraints. To them it was a silent, cheerless, smileless day, from the morning hour of its dawn until the little sufferers gladly sought their pillows, enlivened with the thought that six long days of sinful frolic with ball, marble and kite must intervene before they should again be called upon to perform monastic penance.

The Knickerbocker life was in perfect keeping with its Sabbath—steady, determined, conventional industry was its prime characteristic element, assured competency its aim, quiet contentment its goal. No doubtful speculative projects were entertained; "*Chevalliers d'Industrie*," few and far between, were looked upon with distrust. Moderate in tastes and studiously frugal in their expenditure of the dollars amassed by honest toil, our ancestors had but few rivalries to disturb their equanimity, and these were not of the costly kind which to-day call for such fearful twistings and turnings on the part of aspiring New Yorkers to effect a balance between the means and the ends. Fashion ruled, as she ever has, since Mother Eve glanced at the reflection of her beauty as it was mirrored by the placid waters of Eden, but the usually exacting mistress seemed to assimilate herself to the moderate views of the simple men and women among whom her lot was temporarily cast. Her demands for changes and variety were very limited and her exactness confined to decorous substantial neatness. Though the prescribed style of attire would be considered a marvel of hideousness to-day, still all dressed as if in uniform, from head to foot; so to have laughed at the custom of your neighbor would virtually be tantamount to jeering at your own, a thing people are not apt to do in sober earnest. The toilets of the ladies were certainly far from being graceful; little calculated to enhance the charm of face or figure, less even than the quaint girls of the shaker Quakeresses of Lebanon; besides, the flat, broad, heelless buskin, or the prunella slipper were very unattractive affairs when viewed in contrast with the natty walking boot and its tapering heel, now so bewitchingly displayed on our promenades. But then we knew no other mode, and were compelled to be satisfied with the means within reach to gratify our circumscribed desires for display. In this at least our progenitors were happier than their successors: that they were not rendered supremely wretched by the insatiate longings now so painfully apparent in cosmopolitan New York, for respectable comfort, attained by patient striving, fully satisfied their highest aspirations. Whether their limited views of the pleasure and happiness which this life should afford, were correct, might be a difficult question to argue with those of our day, whose lives have been and are one continuous round of giddy excitement, who look upon labor, in any form, as degrading; who have adopted as their motto, "*Dum vivamus, vivamus*," and who are now reaping the abundant harvest which their prudent ancestors so carefully planted, and are scattering it broadcast in wasteful extravagance and riotous living.

It is becoming, nay it is a duty one owes to one's self and to the society in which our lot is cast, to live up to the times, to conform in moderation to usages and customs; in fine so to demean ourselves as to appear before our fellows "*sans reproche*" in dress and appointments. Here we claim ends our public obligation to the outside world, and we have long marvelled that the powerful press of New York has been so studiously silent on the subject of this wicked extravagance —this crime of fashion which now pervades all classes, absorbing the energy and sapping the very vitals of the coming generation. We claim as a right and duty to put in an appearance in vindication of a better taste and more modest expenditure. It may happen that in so doing we invade the established monarchy of Fashion and thereby give serious offense to some high priests and priestesses who worship at her shrine, but we profess to be too well versed in the true and beautiful to hesitate in what we conceive to be a manly duty; so we place annulus in the lists, resolved to splinter a lance and war against this crying error of judgment which is fast running into licentiousness. Through the great thoroughfares of our city, *fashion* rolls along in one steady stream of wealth and witchery, of waste and want. Her votaries saunter past, or recline in costly equipages wrapped in Indian shawls, for the possession of which the East India Company, in the days of Warren Hastings, would have waged war against a regiment of native princes. We will not say "up town," but speaking generally, will assert the fact, that with masses expense is outrunning income, and that income is sought after in channels which too often have their source in fraud, and find their issue where crime is wedded to punishment, and punishment to perpetual infamy. In and out of the great silken and dry goods warehouses, in and out of the tempting doorways of the golconda jewelry establishments, where diamonds sparkle with more temptation in their pendant glory than did the apple in the Garden of Paradise; crowds pass in and out, with the spirit of determined rivalry within flushed faces, the petty spirit to outvie one the other in the display of bracelets, of gorgeous pins, cameos of fabulous price, bills of destructive items. How exquisite is woman, appropriately, modestly attired: how radiant are her eyes when there is no imperial bauble to dash a rival splendor. A rosebud half hid upon the veiled bosom, a stray curl dancing on a chaste brow; a dainty shawl, whose modest colors do not blush at their own price; a modest robe, whose mysterious undulations teach us to look upon the wearer as a being of perfected taste and dignified modesty, and challenges the honest admiration of every true-hearted gentleman. How our hearts yearn towards her as we feel that she is a woman, not a doll; a wife, not a flirt; a maid, and not a decked temptation; a wife who would guard her husband's credit "on change" as she would his honor at home; a maid whose whole deportment singles her as the fit companion for life of a conscientious, upright man: a companion, without a wish for liveries, with no sigh for foreign dances of arousing intoxication in saloons where the glitter illumes her father's haggard face, as he reflects that on the morrow when he reaches his place of business the expense of all this reckless display will be handed him in a bill, the footing of which will shake his credit and perhaps cast him on the world a ruined man. We would not disturb, but would rather encourage the social enjoyments of this great city. We would not deprive those who enjoy them of the many evening gatherings, the plenteous spread of republican hospitality, the beauty and perfume of home-raised flowers or home-bred loveliness; but we would now and forever enter a solemn protest against this pride of dress, this useless extravagance, this rage for corrupt expenditure. Is there any heartfelt satisfaction or sincerity in the pre-puffed entertainment which Mrs. Crœsus is to give to-morrow night at her palatial mansion? Is there much enjoyment in the anticipation of an entertainment which is to cost the poor devil of a stock-jobbing husband most of the profits of his hap-hazard speculations? Not a bit of it. The shining moire antique, the costly lace, the regal gem, the contraband boquet, received by stealth from some famed gallant, may pass muster for a time in a crowded saloon; but, Madame Crœsus, you must come to grief in the end no matter to what extent you have strained your extravagance, for *Madame Nouveau Riche* will surely cross your path, and you will find yourself in an eclipse. Her scarf alone cost thousands, the plume that decks her chignon was the gift of a Russian prince, her tiny fingers bear the tribute of a dozen lovers, each worth its weight in forgery and fraud. For mercy's sake, fair and beloved American ladies, do set your faces against this reckless riot in extravagant display, this *Vanity Fair*. Turn your thoughts inwardly for a moment and reflect. Serious thought may perhaps induce some to exercise that moderation which will commend itself even in this railroad age. Vie not with the mushrooms that spring up in a night, and wither if they be not promptly gathered. The test of social elevation is a moderate tone of conduct, for that marks a mind secure in its own strength and equal to the destiny to which Heaven has invoked it.

Genuine hospitality was a prominent feature of Knickerbocker life. The old fogies had hearts, and big at that, though their carefulness would now be set down as parsimony, but their sympathies and their pleasures clustered around the family hearth in winter and the family porch in summer. *Home* was the family castle; it was the stronghold to which even the offshoots clung, and in time of trouble it afforded a sure refuge for all the worthy ones who raised the brass knocker. It was reared upon a sure foundation and frugal forethought was the bolt employed to bar the entrance against harassing and wasting cares. Order, punctuality and cleanliness were its chief ornaments, and it was ever ruled by a parental authority strictly enforced. There was no lack of social enjoyment within its enclosure, but even that was tempered by a moderation which precluded the idea of satiety. The tables of our forefathers were simple in appointments, yet they were bountifully provided when the limited variety which the markets afforded was considered. The meal consisted of one course, or rather the repast comprising meats, poultry, vegetables, pies, puddings, sweetmeats and *fruits* (viz.: Newtown pippins, almonds and raisins) was crowded upon the board with such artistic arrangement as circumstances would permit. As extension tables had not then been introduced, considerable figuring had to be indulged in before the blue china platters could be placed so as to allow sufficient space for the full display of the French gilt edged tea set which was the matron's pride. The viands on these grand occasions, when perchance the Dominie, Doctor or some other dignitary was to honor the house with his company, were prepared or directly superintended by the dame in person, as those duties were deemed too important to be performed by a deputy and far too delicate to be executed by a menial. In this connection there comes up a vivid recollection,—grandmother's pantry. To us youngsters it appeared the storehouse of everything that mortal man could either desire or hope for to make life a perfect Elysian. That pantry has its charms even now in fancy as its many dainties are recalled. Notwithstanding some sage modern philosopher has discovered the astounding fact that the man who sighs to taste once more such pies as his mother made, would be sadly disappointed, were his wish granted, to find he was sadly mistaken, as he had lost his youthful appetite. That idea is only " a weak invention of the enemy." In any event grandmother's pantry would be a curiosity to our city ladies who are accustomed to the convenient market and grocery, restaurant or confectioner's shop, from which at a moment's notice any needed article of necessity or luxury can be obtained. Grandmother had no such reserve from which to draw her supplies in case of emergency, but was compelled to rely upon those famous pantry shelves to furnish the needful supplies or the few extra dainties deemed essential to the proper entertainment of guests. Groceries, in the old-fashioned meaning of the word, constituted the bulk of the treasures hoarded within the tabooed enclosure of that mysterious receptacle. The door was carefully locked as a sure precaution against the inquisitive eyes and quick fingers of the household hopefuls, who were ever on the alert for a sly peep and grab should the cautious guardian chance for a moment to leave the door ajar. Flour, sugar, coffee, tea, with boxes of soap and starch, formed the grand staples of the semi-annual supply, and were ranged on the ample floor with mathematical precision. The first wide shelf above these prominent essentials was devoted to the tin spice boxes duly labeled as to their several contents, with sundry large earthen jars which were well known to contain the plain cake for daily use, while carefully behind them were stored, as a precautionary measure, a couple of similar receptacles, which were special objects of interest, as they hid from view the best pound and plum cake, a bit of which was now and then awarded as the reward of extraordinary virtue, but was especially dedicated to such occasions when it was deemed absolutely indispensable to parade "*the company tea set*," the silver tea pot, sugar bowl, milk jug and the little cut glass preserve plates which stood up in a corner, with tissue paper between each, lest they should by accident be scratched by friction. The second shelf was reserved for the *sweetmeats*, which though not so varied in kind, are in memory far more luscious than the pretentious compounds now purchased in their stead by Grandmother's aristocratic descendants. Peach, plum, quince about complete the list, but the fruits were carefully selected, and loaf sugar unadulterated by chemical science was the only agent employed in their preparation by the skilled housewife in person. Her whole soul was, however, engaged in the work, and her syrup was not to be surpassed in richness or clearness if care and assiduity could prevent. Quality was her aim in sweetmeats as well as her standard in more important matters than those pertaining to mere articles for consumption, though excellence in these was "*sine qua non*" to her conception of good breeding. No baskets of champagne or cases of Rhine wine; no imported sauces, marmalades, pickles, or appetizers were displayed on the shelves, but a moderate supply of Jamaica rum, pure Madeira and French brandy, with a flask of peppermint cordial, were then ever at hand to "welcome the coming or speed the parting guest." In the winter, Newtown pippins mingled their aroma with the other *good things* stored in this house of plenty. One of these *good things* must especially not be overlooked, for it is not seen to-day, save in the window of some confectioner, where it is barely recognizable, though it bears the name still of *peanut candy*. The thin, attenuated paste has but slight resemblance in appearance and does not approach in taste the massive blocks of the spiced delicacy which rose like a monument to bid defiance to the most vigorous attacks of man and boy; but, as plate after plate was hammered off to meet the demand created by the bright circle congregated around the cheerful hickory blaze, it disappeared ere the long Winter had lapsed into Spring. Here and there, at prominent points on the shelves, were displayed ancient family heir-looms in the crockery line, preserved as mementoes to recall some favorite set which had succumbed to the ravages of time. Grandmother took great pride in regaling our young eyes with an occasional inspection of these much revered "*penates*," many of them having been special transmissions from the far-off, dusty past. Their separate histories, as received from her lips, invested each plate, cup or saucer with a consideration which bordered upon veneration, and we considered them as actual witnesses to a long line of worthy ancestry. Grandmother's pantry was a fact in youth; it is still, as it were, palpable in middle age, for having once been seen and known can never be forgotten, but will hold its place in memory, despite all the modern appliances and lazy counterfeits which increased wealth and luxury have introduced in its stead. These, as they pass away to give place to newer inventions, which pander more and more to inertia and sloth, have no charm upon which recollection loves to linger; they fix no bright spot in childhood's days.

Grandmother's parlor will appear very indigent, common place and perchance poverty-stricken, to such as have known no other than the richly appointed, luxurious drawing rooms, now deemed so essential to comfort, and actually demanded by respectability. The stiff, high-backed, armless mahogany chairs, covered with shiny black haircloth fastened to the ponderous frames by brass-headed nails, thickly set, all **ranged at precise distances**, plumb against the wall, *like sentinels at a present;* the long, narrow, hard sofa, with seat so round, unyielding and slippery, that it afforded capital *coasting* for youngsters, when the lynx-eyed guardian of the sacred domain was too busily employed in household duties to check the contraband sport, this sofa would certainly not be claimed a second time as a couch of ease for a fashionable belle to repose on after a night of dissipation; the rolls, which for form's sake were styled pillows, and stuffed in appropriate niches at either end, would have afforded but slight ease to her aching head, for they were as unimpressible as flint; the grand, *best* carpet of the highly-prized *Lilly pattern* with its straggling vines and well-developed leaves of the highest possible green would fail to meet the entire commendation of the eye accustomed to the soft, subdued substance of velvety softness at present in vogue; the high broad *mantle tree* of gaily variegated Italian marble would be looked upon as a waste of raw material when viewed side by side with the elaborately chiseled resting place for statuettes which ornaments the modern *salon;* the china vases mounted on pedestals and filled with artificial roses, as unlike nature as man could possibly make them; the tall, highly-polished silver candle-sticks, flanked by the inseparable snuffers and tray rubbed bright to match; the old-fashioned sideboard with heavy stubby decanters filled with Madeira and Santa Cruz, and its silver baskets each day replenished with fresh doughnuts and crullers as a real earnest of hospitality; the stationary pier tables at the extremities, special places of deposit for the family Bible, a volume or two of some well-authenticated commentaries and a copy of Watt's hymns, which books were the mainstay of the household so far as library was concerned – as the venerable, if not to say venerated New York *Observer* furnished weekly all the desired information on missionary subjects which were then deemed of paramount importance to a community so supremely happy and contented; the diminutive, thin-legged, wheezy piano, purchased during some paroxysm of thoughtless extravagance, but never opened save on the semi-annual dusting day; the indispensable rocking-chair and foot-stool; the portraits of grandfather and grandmother as they were supposed to have presented themselves in their far-off youth to the artistic eye of some traveling painter; they were mementoes of the fact that a marriage had taken place, and served to transmit some faint idea of a long defunct costume; a worsted work sampler, commemorative of some solemn church yard reminiscence or the more common Ten Commandments, the crowning effort of a much-beloved, departed daughter, having been named, the ordinary array of decoration is complete, with the single exception that the bright green, inside Venetian blinds so essential to completeness of detail were for the moment forgotten, but thank goodness the oversight was discovered in time to avoid giving a pang to some ancient dame, who had dusted and shaded them for so many years that she would not easily have pardoned this prominent negligence on the part of one who professes to narrate facts and describe things as they were.

CHAPTER THIRD.

Many of the quaint pieces of furniture which were grandmother's pride are still sound and firm, for they were made "*not for a day, but for all time*," but they are rarely seen save on moving day, when, with much tugging and many a half suppressed—thought, they are borne by unappreciative hands from one garret, together with dust and cobwebs, into another, until such time as the words *To Let* are posted on the doorway of their uncertain resting place, for grandmother's descendants have become birds of passage, soon tire of sameness, and have long erased from their lexicon the now practically historic word "home." Still, on a sharp winter night there was solid comfort and unfeigned enjoyment in that primitive old parlor. The oak logs piled high on the massive andirons, blazing and crackling, dispensed a most genial warmth; the astral lamp and wax candles shed a subdued, mellow light. At such a time the stiff high chairs were not amiss when drawn cosily about the spacious fire-place, and the family convened for social chat. Nuts and apples, cider and doughnuts, with grandfathers Santa Cruz toddy, comprised the entertainment. On such festive occasions the bashful sweetheart not unfrequently managed to slip in, and while paring apples for the *old folks*, would snatch the opportunity to glance the story of his love, and find himself assured by a crimson blush that would shed a halo about the prim old parlor. The simple unostentatious home has at length passed away, but long years have been required to eradicate the lessons it inculcated, and the staid habits formed by its punctuality and decorum. The barriers which encircled it were firmly reared, but have now been leveled by worldly pride, aided by all the forces luxury could marshal to affect their downfall. The splendid palaces erected by modern *Aladdins* now constitute one of the crowning glories of our beautiful city; they are magnificent to look upon, as row upon row springs up as if by magic—they are indeed undisputed types of skilled labor. But the query starts almost unbidden, are not most of them costly piles reared on the "*ignis fatuus*" of unsubstantial theory and doubtful bubble, which may at any moment enforce their transfer from the possession of the vain reputed owners into the stern clutches of the tyrant *Mortgage?* when the gay occupants who revelled in their credit, based on hope alone, will find themselves quickly forgotten in the race for notoriety which now sweeps over Manhattan.

THE BATTERY.

The Battery was our "breathing spot," and its charms were chanted with the same pride and delight now manifested by young New York when descanting on the splendors which cluster in and about the Central Park. Its graveled shady paths and somewhat irregular plots of grass had not been superintended by a professor educated in the science of landscape gardening, nor was the enclosure under the special care of a "high commission." Still no modern art or set of men possessed the power to add to the natural beauties of its surroundings, as the eye swept over our unrivalled bay, any more than could such human agencies supply the life giving breeze, which on each afternoon was freely wafted from old Ocean, to cool the fevered city. It could boast of no statues, it had no sequestered bowers or artistic fountains, no mall with its music, no lake with its gondolas, no deer, buffalo, camel or Merino sheep, its benches were rude, unpainted boards, admirably adapted to tell the finish of a new penknife, and yet lacking all these and many more of the newly discovered necessities of the present hour, it was to us a park of unequaled beauty, and travelers from distant shores were loud in its praises, though their recollection of far famed Naples was vividly fresh. The Battery was our summer promenade, when it was no bar to social standing for a family to remain in the city, for even the belle or gallant did not lose caste by declining to participate in the routine of watering place life, simple and inexperienced as it then was. We had summer resorts in those days, and they were patronized by the best and most prominent citizens of the country. The springs at Saratoga were resorted to, primarily for their restorative qualities, but the visitors who sought them, very far from playing the role of confirmed invalids, made their sojourn there a season of rational temperate enjoyment, which enabled them to return to their duties reinvigorated in mind as well as in body, anxious for the renewal of the pleasant associations then formed, when another year should have rolled away. "*The Beach at Rockaway,*" immortalized by the military poet, Geo. P. Morris, was another and more accessible resort where New Yorkers were wont to congregate, while the now much despised Coney Island, with its broiled chicken, its roast clams, and salt sea waves, lured many a party to its unpretending hotel. No serious preparations were requisite for the pleasure trips; no scrimpings or curtailments needed on the part of father or mother to fill Saratoga trunks with dresses, or liquidate extortionate charges. Marriages were more decorously brought about; flirtations more innocent and far less expensive to all parties concerned.

"*As the Sun went down—*" No, not exactly then, for one of the maxims of the day was "*Early to bed and early to rise*," but when the Sun was far past its meridian power, the best, the bravest and the fairest of our denizens wended their way to the Battery to enjoy a stroll and exchange friendly greetings. It was in reality a pleasure ground, the leveling hand of greedy speculation had not touched it, and it was removed from the dust and turmoil of traffic. Private residences as pretentious as any the city then possessed flanked it on the North and East, on the South and West the grand old Bay glistened and danced. The yacht with its symmetrical lines, its raking masts, its cloud of snowy canvas, its club house, commodore, regatta, cup, its balls and signals, its nautical lore and international pride was then in the *periauger* and cat-boat state of existence. The *"America"* had neither been designed nor launched, but George Steers was perhaps whittling chips into the curving shapes which eventually gave to his name a world-wide fame. The *oar* was then, however, in its glory, unstained by the gambling matches which in latter days have fastened themselves upon this manly invigorating sport. *The Wave*, with her famous four-oared crew, was the champion boat of the hour. The Rollins and Dunderdale Brothers were the athletes whose powerful, steady stroke achieved her renown; and the hearty plaudits of promenaders were freely awarded them when displaying their masterly skill they sent their tiny shell at a racing pace over the waters.

Castle Garden, the legend says, was created to protect the city against the foreign invader. Whether these invaders were to be New Jersey Indians, armed with bow and arrow, or Staten Island pirates, bent upon destruction with popgun and firecracker, is not related; but it is certain very limited force would have been required to effect an entrance through its brick walls. About the time we write of, its "loud-mouthed" armament had been removed; it had been placed by special orders from somewhere on a peace footing. It was neither a concert saloon, an opera house or a receptacle for needy emigrants, but the old white-washed barn was devoted to the restaurant business on a very limited scale, as ice cream, lemonade and sponge cake constituted the list of the delicacies from which to select. The ticket of admission required to pass its *portcullis* cost one shilling; but that was a mere form instituted to guarantee perfect decorum, for it was redeemable as cash in exchange for either of the above-specified articles of refreshment. At the close of a Summer day its *frowning battlements* were crowded with listeners, eager to catch a strain of martial music wafted from Governor's Island. The Battery possessed another grand attraction, and one which has been excluded from the Central Park: it was the favorite parade ground of our famous militia, then under the command of Major General Morton. The official and domestic headquarters of this dignitary were situated on State Street, and as the veteran clung to his honors long after age had rendered him too infirm to mount his charger, the *crack* corps of the division at intervals paid their commander the compliment of a marching salute, to be reviewed from his balcony; and at the same time win the smiles of beauty as a reward for their gallant bearing. Conspicuous among these military organizations were the Tompkins Blues, Captain Vincent, and the Pulaski Cadets, Captain McArdle. A fierce rivalry existed between these two commands, and when either paraded it was certain to be accompanied by a *side-walk* committee of admiring sympathizers and imposing numbers. So far as the public could judge, both were composed "of good men and true;" they were natty and neat in their soldierly make-up; they certainly marched with the determined, precise tread of veterans who had been under fire and would not flinch. Sure it was, both had an undisputed reputation for charging upon a well-loaded board with a will that left no tell-tale vestige. "The *esprit du corps*," so characteristic of their early career, has been in a measure transmitted to their successors, who keep alive the strife for supremacy under the titles of Light and City Guards respectively. But the veterans of the rival factions, enfeebled by excessive gastronomical service; no longer able to cope with the fresh recruits, have enrolled themselves as a band of brothers, and by special legislative enactment assumed the imposing title of the *Old Guard*. By special order of their chosen commandant, the now venerable George W. McLean, these scarred warriors meet now and then, clad in full regalia, to fight their battles over again; to pledge each other in sparkling bumpers, with "no heel taps," in commemoration of Old Lang Syne, and to close up the ranks, as one after another falls by the way in this battle of life.

The streets bordering on and adjacent to the Battery were the choice spots of abode. Commerce in its imperative demand for space at length drove off the reluctant proprietors, and this once favorite lounging place dwindled by neglect into a barren waste, visited by few save the homeless emigrants who sought shelter in the barracks at Castle Garden, and the lawless vagrant who prowled about to plunder the friendless stranger just landed on our shores. Many of the original houses still remain, but have passed through all the stages of decline which mark city neighborhoods when tabooed by *Fashion*.

At the corner of Broadway and Marketfield Street there still stands the outward presentment of a once famous mansion, which now bears the sign of Washington Hotel. In former years it was the residence of Sir Henry Clinton, and noted for its generous hospitality. But its light went out, when Edward Prime, of the well-known banking house of Prime, Ward & King, who tenaciously clung to it as his chosen home, was compelled to abandon it. Stephen Whitney, Phillips Phœnix, Peter H. Schenck, and the Messrs Schermerhorn, Ray, with their confreres, were soon forced to follow suit in the up-town movement, and boarding houses ruled the district where the old stock were born, lived and died.

Before passing on, it would be remiss not to stop in for a moment to exchange civilities with Peter Bayard, a publican all be it, but still a worthy and noted Knickerbocker. On State Street near Pearl there was a famous resort; not famous by virtue of outward appearance, for it was but a simple two-story building. Its modest exterior, however, gave no sign of the glorious cheer which reigned within. Peter Bayard was the presiding genius, and his epicurean fame extended far beyond the contracted city limits; for pompous, portly patrons *from the far off up-river*, with low-crowned, broad-brimmed hats, massive fob chains and seals, cambric ruffles, and spacious coat-flaps; sedate, primly-clad sojourners in the City of Penn, snuff-colored denizens of Jersey, and not a few typical representatives of the *cute notion tribe*, who had heard of the morsels which Peter wrought to tickle the palate, came personally to test their truthfulness. Peter dispensed choice wines and liquors; the rarest bivalves were sure to be found there in season; in fact, he ransacked the market to procure dainties to educate taste. But Peter's crowning effort was *Turtle Soup*, that was the magnet which never failed to draw a full house. It was delicious; even the dim recollections of its savory fumes is tantamount to a feast, when-pitted against the watery substances now served in its stead, even though they be served in gorgeous apartments and the vessels which contain them be of the nearest approach to genuine silver. For years Pete Bayard's was the rendezvous for old and young who cultivated and appreciated the inner man. After a bowl of turtle soup and a glass or two of his generous *Port* as a sure corrective for acidity, every one became a friend of *our* friend Peter Bayard.

CHAPTER FOURTH.

The trade of the city was concentrated at the Southern end of the Island, and as a sequence the hotels were found in that section. They were not numerous, for their patronage in the main depended upon the then limited traveling public, and such bachelors as were forced from circumstances to avail themselves of this pretext for a home. *To board* was not considered *exactly the thing* by the matrons of the period, and the dame who voluntarily abandoned her house-keeping and adopted hotel or boarding-house life in its stead, soon found herself deliberately snubbed, while the one who was compelled by circumstances to submit to this curtailment of *woman's rights*, was heartily commiserated with by her friends at all their tea-party gatherings. Still, despite this positive drawback against hotel life, there was always to be found a fair sprinkling of human kind to enliven the parlor and prevent the dining-room from becoming a mere *feeding trough*. For man was not created to be alone when time began; left to himself even now he would soon degenerate and be contented with husks, if they satiated appetite.

Miss Margaret Mann was the head and front of the noted boarding-house of New York, and as this was largely patronized by the ladies it deserves precedence. No. 61 Broadway was a celebrated locality; its capacity and reputation would perhaps entitle it to be styled a hotel. Aunt Margaret, as the hostess was familiarly styled, was an advanced specimen of her sex. She wore a plain frock, wholly unornamented, and scant as locomotion would permit; no laces, frills, ribbons, bows,—knicknacks of any description, did not find favor in her eyes; she mounted a scrimpy cap on extraordinary occasions, but in full business trim her lank hair was twisted in an unartistic lump at the back of her head, while the balance was forced to make shift with an occasional "lick and promise" hastily bestowed. Aunt Margaret was a driving woman. No one would have dreamed of such nonsense as addressing her in soft, soothing tones, for the result would have proved about as satisfactory should some fool attempt to pat and flatter a locomotive under a full head of steam. Compliment or suavity were not in her vocabulary. Brusque and bustling, she was never known to rest, and rumor says she gave but little to her hard-worked employees. She was thick-set and heavy in person, yet she seemed ubiquitous, and no detective, even old Hays himself, could surpass her prying qualities. She was rarely demonstrative, but was known to possess a tongue which when called into requisition was a most powerful weapon either for offense or defence as the case might be. Woe betide the unlucky wight who provoked her wrath, for when fully roused she respected neither person, time nor place.

But under Aunt Margaret's hard exterior there was hidden a well of human kindness which occasionally bubbled up and demonstrated that the fountain at her heart had not run dry. To her own she was gentle and kind. To an aged mother and three orphan children of a deceased sister, she was peculiarly attached, and her usually cold eye would light up with sympathetic pride when these were noticed by her guests; but to no one save these children, and a few of their young companions, did she ever betray the feelings which are generally attributed to woman. The house itself, beyond being eminently respectable, and so to speak, fashionable, had but little to recommend it. The parlors were plainly furnished and dimly lighted; the bedrooms scantily supplied with the commonest articles of necessity; the long dining-hall, lighted from either side by a row of naked, staring windows, unadorned with white walls; narrow tables furnished with a goodly variety of palatably prepared food, but set out with cheap crockery, cheap glass, cheap everything which tends to render a meal attractive; yet it was accepted by strangers of note, foreign and native. The guests of the house were, as a rule, sociable, perhaps from necessity, for the circle of amusements were limited, and so men were satisfied to enjoy themselves with a dance and an occasional song. It was in the parlor of 61 Broadway that Sinclair, the father of Mrs. Edwin Forrest, actually made his debut in America, for on the eve of his first appearance at the Park Theatre he delighted his listeners with the strains of the "Mistletoe Bough," a ballad which stamped his popularity with our lovers of music during his prolonged engagement. Tyrone Power, when here, was also a guest at this house, and enchanted all who met him with his rich, polished brogue, and rollicking fascination of manner. On the whole, Aunt Margaret had seldom cause to find fault with her patrons, but now and then, when some interloper would accidentally slip in, she soon discovered some summary method to dispense with the company of the objectionable inmate.

The City Hotel occupied the entire front of the block on Broadway bounded by Thames and Cedar Streets. It was not only the most celebrated house of entertainment in the city but travelers asserted it had no equal in the United States. So far as architecture was concerned it was a plain, high structure, pierced with the usual number of square windows, unadorned by lace or damask hangings, with nothing, in fact, to exclude the rays of Old Sol or the impertinent glances of inquisitive neighbors but solid white inside shutters, most effectual bars against both light and air. The interior fittings of our *Grand Hotel*, whose register paraded the names of our most prominent citizens from every section, in addition to those of the limited number of travelers and tourists from abroad, who were sufficiently enterprising to brave the tedious passage across the boisterous Atlantic, were very plain when compared with the gilded, frescoed palaces, adorned by every article of *vertu* which the cunning artificers of the old and new world can devise to pander to an extravagant era. The furniture was the best of its kind, durable but unostentatious; in perfect keeping with the modest views which then ruled. Substantial comfort, so far as it could be had, was the ruling motive, and in no instance was that paramount essential ever lost sight of to make room for senseless display. The dining-room of the City Hotel was spacious, light and well ventilated, but its appointments could lay claim to little, save the most thorough neatness, and scrupulous cleanliness. The waiters, ample as to numbers, were well trained and obsequiously attentive to every want, and the guest would have been more than unreasonable who found fault with a feast abundant in quantity and selected with the greatest care by the most experienced caterer in the land. Our markets were not bare of delicacies, for our *bay* and *rivers* furnished fish in every variety and as delicate in flavor as they are conceded to be at present; wild duck and game of every sort abounded within limited distance; meats were plentiful and cheap, and, with the single exception of mutton, most excellent in quality. But, so far as fruits and vegetables were concerned, the supply beyond the commonest sorts was very limited, and that confined to the season when they could be raised out of doors in the immediate vicinity. The tomato, now so general an article of consumption, was unknown as an edible and grown merely as an ornamental plant in country gardens, where it was styled "love apple" by the agricultural dames.

Dinner has, however, always been a most important daily event with all classes and conditions of men, women and children. In the early days of our city the noon hour was devoted by the plodding burghers to the enjoyment of the noontide feast. When the old Middle Dutch bell clanked twelve o'clock, work was suspended, as if "the affairs of men" had come to a full stop; master and man quit without compliment, each hastening to his abode to devote the prescribed respite to the positive refreshment of his important person. Lunch is a very modern word, so far as New York is concerned. Three meals per diem, and to be partaken of at home at specified periods, was the rule. *Bites* and *nips* were unknown in Knickerbocker parlance; what a man ate or drank, must be shared with his family. There were no convenient "*dives*," a word well understood at present; few eating houses, with "*meals at all hours*" displayed on flaming signs; free lunches not dreamed of; sandwiches only prepared at home, and only on such rare occasions when some protracted journey of several hours duration was necessarily undertaken. Breakfast, dinner and tea, at the specified hour, was prepared at *home*, and absence from either, or even a dilatory appearance, was deemed just cause for a domestic court martial, and if of frequent recurrence, worthy a sympathetic meeting of condolence by the watchful neighbors.

When the City Hotel was in its full prime, some glimmering rays of modern improvement were introduced by one and another, who after visiting England and France, had returned home inoculated with what was then contemptuously styled "*foreign airs.*" Some of these hooted at the primitive noon-meal so hugely enjoyed in their unpolished youth, and by slow stages three o'clock became the extra fashionable limit for a meal called dinner, for it crowded so closely upon the old Knickerbocker tea, that the innovation was disputed inch by inch, as our Grandmother's prerogative of a long undisturbed afternoon was in a fair way of being wiped out by this new-fangled change in domestic life.

The City Hotel was among the first to fall into line and three o'clock was announced as its dinner hour, though a noon table was spread for the accommodation of such thoroughbred sticklers as would not conform. As most of the guests were business men, the change, however, was of slight consequence, as these would not at any hour of the day have devoted the time to the discussion of a repast so essential to good digestion. Dyspepsia always has been an American weakness; all the Trollopes and Dickens of the world cannot eradicate this national trait. It may be said that New Yorkers, especially, love dyspepsia; at any rate they court it from their cradles to their graves. The choice viands of the City Hotel table were dealt with in the most summary manner, as the hungry partakers were compelled to hasten back to store, counting-house or office to resume the broken thread of traffic.

There were, however, a few choice spirits, bachelors or widowers, heaven only knows which, who had drifted, one by one, within the portals of the City Hotel, where, by similarity of tastes, they had formed a coterie of their own, and after passing the needful by-laws they had become a mutual admiration society. They clustered at a specified spot, of which they had formally taken possession, and each day settled themselves to enjoy to the full of their bent the evening of their days.

They were men who had lived beyond the time when drudgery was a prime necessity, and by common consent they lingered at the table after the heat of the battle for food was over, to crack their jokes, nibble their filberts, and sip their wine.

The wine cellar of the Old Hotel was a well-known institution, and its memory is still cherished by not a few, who in youth had tasted its rare stores. Its shelves were loaded tier upon tier with the choicest vintages the nicest taste could call, and the selections were pronounced by connoisseurs as unsurpassed in purity or flavor. The judgment then expressed was in after years amply verified; for when the old stamping-ground was abandoned in consequence of the *up-town* movement, the remnants remaining of the favorite brands were secured at fabulous prices by the initiated. Light wines from the Rhine and clarets from France were not then in vogue, even the now indispensable Heidseck was but little affected, as the taste ran to the more generous, fruity and invigorating Madeira, port and sherry of a quality and perfume which gold cannot purchase now. In these rare juices of the grape, the bevy of old "*bon vivants*" delighted to indulge, and it was rare sport to watch them as a bottle of some rare variety was carefully uncorked by Chester Jennings in person; it was a perfect study to note the genuine glow of expectation that mantled the ruddy faces of the group as each daintily raised his glass, that the eye might revel once more in the glorious tint ere the full fruition of taste should impart perfect earthly bliss.

This band of "jolly good fellows," who lingered day after day for long years over their wine and nuts, were well known characters in the city, and were especially familiar to such as visited the City Hotel where they lived and died. A mere mention of some of their names with a brief description of their peculiarities will bring back many pleasing recollections to any one familiar with the men who figured in Gotham forty years ago.

Colonel Nick Saltus, a retired merchant of wealth and a confirmed old bachelor, was the acknowledged chairman and spokesman of the peculiar group. In person he was short and thickset, with a manner so pompous, that once seen, the man was for all time photographed upon the recollection. His tone of voice was unusually abrupt and dictatorial, and until mollified by his duck and olives, accompanied with copious libations of Maleira, he might with the greatest propriety be characterized as *thundering* cross. His dress was singular, rather from his method of donning it than from any special departure from the prevailing mode. His costume as a rule consisted of a brown frock coat with velvet collar buttoned closely at the throat, a black handkerchief, stiff standing shirt collar reaching to the ears. His gold spectacles were balanced on the very tip of his well-cultivated nose, a formidable feature, by the way, of his closely-shaven face, while his high beaver was canted so far to the front as completely to overshadow his eyes. His carriage was wonderfully erect, and he walked with the strut of a dandy up to his very latest promenade. The

Colonel worshipped himself, but his little vanities were harmless, and his hauteur soon gave way when one had the patience to listen with respectful silence to the long-drawn details of his youthful indiscretions and gallant exploits. For many years his migrations were limited by Cedar Street on the North and Wall Street on the South; his aim being to have a good time and in his own way, which was systematic in the extreme; and each day closed like its predecessor: the worthy colonel was, at or about ten p. m., considerably "how come you so," when fortified with a generous bumper of spiced rum for a nightcap, the old fellow toddled off to bed.

Werckmeister was the Colonel's right bower at table, but was unlike him in every particular as it was possible for man to be. Tall, sedate, quiet in dress and address he was a fine representative of the German gentleman. There are but few citizens not familiar with the old sign, "Werckmeister, Importer of Toys," which, until very recently, was conspicuously displayed at the northeast corner of Broadway and Liberty Street, between which point and the City Hotel its proprietor migrated with marvellous punctuality for more than a quarter of a century. A bachelor like the Colonel, his whole time up to three o'clock was devoted to the traffic in which he had accumulated a competency, but all desire for further gain was thrown aside when the all-important dinner hour was at hand. "Its near three o'clock; Werckmeister is on his way to dinner!" was daily the inward exclamation of many a belated man or boy who encountered him in his stereotype tramp from duty to pleasure. The dining-room was the only place in the hotel that he ever frequented; from habit he slept at his store until the day of his death, which occurred when he was far advanced in years. He loved to linger over the dinner table listening to the chat of his companions, and if he ever spoke, the tone was so subdued as to be inaudible amid the boisterous conversation of his boon companions. Having no kindred in this land of his adoption, he never was known to mingle in any society save such as he met at the City Hotel table, and with that his limited desires seemed fully satisfied.

Hollingsworth, a third notable in this set, was an enigma to every one unacquainted with the man and his history. In appearance he was shrivelled and pinched, and had grown old and infirm in the hotel of which he had become a permanent fixture. For years he never left the house, and found occupation in self-imposed duties which he never neglected. Possessed of abundant means he denied himself no comfort or luxury, yet he seemingly relied upon the proprietors with the simplicity of a child, and called upon them at all times as though he were the recipient of their bounty. The reading-room was his special care and hobby; the newspapers claimed his undivided attention. Up betimes in the morning, he carefully filed each paper as thrown in by the carrier, in its appropriate place; all, save one, and that one was the young, rollicking *Herald*, which the old fellow slyly secured in the hope that it might contain some sweet morsel of scandal with which to regale the chosen circle at their morning meal. The evening journals received the same consideration at his hands; while during the day he occupied himself in smoothing any crumpled sheet which had been carelessly tossed about. This simple task was his only occupation for many years, and was not wholly relinquished until he had become too feeble from advanced age to quit his apartment. At times he was inclined to be chatty, and on a fine afternoon he presented a picture of calm content, as seated on the front stoop backed by the presence of the gay Colonel, he regaled himself by inspecting the panorama of fashion which filed past the door.

CHAPTER FIFTH.

Captain Barker, another prominent character in this old-fashioned group, will be readily recalled. He was a large, heavily-built man, scrupulously neat and methodical in his sable attire, and withal so grave and dignified in his bearing that he would have proved a treasure to the most straight laced sect in Christendom. When actively engaged in the personal happiness of discussing the delicacies of the *cuisine* he sometimes betrayed the fact that even he was afflicted by terrestrial weaknesses; nay, the fact was almost established beyond doubt when with flushed visage he called for a further supply of Harmony Amontillado; but, aside from these occasional moments of forgetfulness, he was apparently absorbed in some grand scheme having in view the amelioration of his race at large. He probably had no nearly allied kindred, for, though rich, no one seemed to claim relationship. For hours he would sit almost motionless at one of the reading-room windows, apparently unconscious of the bustle without; and when casually addressed he would respond with a patronising air, which had the effect of bringing the conversation to an abrupt termination. The Captain affected to disbelieve the post-prandial yarns of the Colonel, and to despise the frivolous jokes he habitually indulged in ; he even now and then exchanged glances of deep disgust with the placid Holingsworth, yet it was by no means infrequent that the deep bass *guffaw* of the solemn Barker stimulated the laughter of these ancient revellers.

The Trans-Atlantic packet ships, which sailed twice each month for European ports, were objects of the greatest importance, and, as a matter of course, their commanders were rated as far above men in the ordinary walks of life. These personages had made our clippers the pride of the city, and as we loved to call it, the envy of the maritime powers of the Old World. Marshall, Holdridge, Cartoff, Johnston, Lines, Ainsworth, Funk and their confrères, were men in whom every confidence was reposed, at a time when the passage to Europe was not the holiday jaunt it is to-day, in this age of floating steam palaces. Then the captains were the chosen guardians to whose care were committed the invalid wife, the timid daughter, the infirm parent, compelled to risk the perils of a long uncertain voyage in search of health, or from other cause of dire necessity, and so momentous a step was the voyage then considered that relations to the third and fourth remove flocked to the dock to bid a tearful adieu to the adventurers. Many of the captains made the City Hotel their headquarters when in port, and their company was eagerly sought by the veteran band. They were all on the "*qui vive*" when a fresh arrival was announced from Sandy Hook, and they would proceed in a body to the Battery to obtain the first glimpse of some boon companion who had been charged with a momentous commission to procure some gastronomical luxury which was anxiously awaited. On the second floor of the hotel there was a spacious and somewhat pretentious apartment, called the Ladies' Dining Room, primarily devoted to the use of families who were traveling or such ladies as were visiting the City for a limited stay. Its high arched ceiling was more than usually grand, and it was decorated with three glass chandeliers deemed marvels of extravagance. Dancing was indulged in to a very moderate extent in New York; the pastime was discountenanced by the church, and if not condemned as absolutely improper, the majority who valued repose, and had no peculiar longing for lectures on immodest levity, chose to forego any participation in the mazy dance, which consisted at the best only of a humdrum cotillion with occasional indulgence in the excitement of the Spanish dance, which would now be considered about as exhilarating as would be a glass of insipid orgeat to an inveterate toper. As a matter of course with such a state of affairs in the dancing line, ball rooms were few, and as the Ladies' Dining was both central and its surroundings eminently respectable, it was on rare occasions converted into a "*salon de dance.*" These decorous assemblages were not denominated Balls, but were announced as *Publicks*, a queer idea of somebody, for they were not public in any sense, the attendance being limited to the pupils, male and female, of John Charruaud, *the Dancing Master* of New York for more than half a century; and their much respected parents, who came not only to watch with pride the graceful undulation of their offspring, but also to see to it that no levity was indulged in. For years Charruaud used this room for instruction; in fact, up to the time when he built his celebrated ball room on White Street between Church and Chapple Streets, on the very borders of civilization. This enterprise was at the time deemed extra-hazardous, so far as speculation was concerned, but the Professor lived and grew rich in his vocation long years after the city had swept past his advanced step; he saw the neighborhood in which his hobby was built rise, flourish and decay, and his pet assembly room become a dog pit, where nightly assembled the scum of European vagabondism.

This useful dining room occasionally was hired for concert purposes by artists from abroad, who by some accident had gleaned the important information that there were dollars in New York. Among those who came to test this fact was Henry Russell, an English Jew, who gave a series of very successful entertainments at the City Hotel. Educated musicians of the time pronounced him a humbug, but his off-hand manner and peculiar style of song took with the public, and he left our shores with a well-filled purse. His voice was of very limited compass, and he introduced a peculiar order of ballad admirably adapted to its peculiarities, and claimed to be the composer of the music. Prominent among his most popular songs were " Wind of the Winter's Night," " The Ivy Green," " The

Maniac," "Come, Brothers, Arouse," and "Woodman Spare that Tree." "Woodman Spare that Tree" was composed by George P. Morris, at the time a literary, military, society notability of the city, and, moreover, in connection with Theodore S. Fay and N. P. Willis, he was the editor of the *Mirror*, the standard weekly of the North. Morris was human, and not a little elated by the popularity of his song, and therefore paid great court to the vocalist who was the means of bringing it so prominently before the public, and, as a consequence, poet and singer frequently met at entertainments, for this Russell became quite a lion in a certain circle. On one occasion, when both were present, Captain Maryatt chanced to be a guest, and Russell was invited to favor the assemblage with the then popular ballad. As he was singing the closing stanza with great pathos the distingtinguished novelist approached the piano and placed before him the following additional verse, written in pencil:

"Lady, give me tea,
    And I will make a bow;
In youth it pleased me,
    And I do love it now;
'Twas my old mother's hand
    That poured it from the pot;
Pray, lady, let it stand
    For it is d——d hot."

The laugh went round as Russell closed. The good-natured poet's pride was deeply wounded, and the genial, mirthful Maryatt saw too late that he had touched our military laureate in a tender spot.

Jennings and Willard were the well-known

proprietors of this far-famed City Hotel. Willard was the prominent partner so far as the guests were concerned. His station was in the office, where from sunrise to midnight he was ever faithful at his post. So marvelous was his activity of mind and body that his complex duties of host, clerk, book-keeper, cashier, bar-keeper, and heaven only knows what besides, were bustled through, not only with apparent ease but with the most unruffled good nature. His world lay within the walls of the City Hotel, as will be abundantly illustrated by a simple but well authenticated anecdote. Billy Niblo, long known to fame by his connection with the prominent amusements of New York, had resolved to abandon his Pine Street "coffee house," and to seek his fortune by opening a suburban place for refreshment and entertainment. Many of his old down-town customers were invited to be present at the opening of the new garden, and among them several who were residents at the City Hotel. They accepted Niblo's courtesy and determined that Willard should make one of their number on the appointed evening. With his accustomed politeness he did not positively decline, so when the time arrived he was duly waited upon and notified of their readiness to start. He smiled his acquiesence, and began fidgeting and bustling around the office, looking first on this shelf and then in that cupboard, but evidently without meeting with the object of his anxious search. At last, giving up in despair, he announced to his friends that for many years he had not been the owner of a hat, and that some one had feloniously abstracted an old beaver which had long lain around awaiting the advent of its rightful owner. Fortunately this unusual predicament could easily be adjusted, for Charles St. John, the celebrated hatter, was directly opposite, and soon supplied the required article, and if still alive will tell of his great surprise when informed that Willard was going out. A hat was procured, and the triumphant party sallied forth in company with the best known man in the city, but who, strange to relate, would have been compelled to inquire his way if he had been placed by himself a stone's throw from the City Hotel. Willard was of short, compact stature; had a well-moulded head, thickly covered with short cropped, wiry grey hair, small quick twinkling eyes, that seemed never at rest. Of an active, cheerful disposition, he had a ready reply to any question, and greeted each new arrival with an assuring smile of welcome. Between him and the traveling public there seemed to exist a bond of sympathetic freemasonry. The secret of this lay in his wonderful memory; a face once seen, a name once scanned on the register seemed to be indelibly fastened upon his mind, and the many stories related of him bearing upon this peculiar trait had great foundation in truth. One well authenticated instance will suffice as an illustration. A gentleman, with nothing peculiar in person, name or position to fix his identity, had been a transient guest of the house, but owing to the serious illness of a favorite child, his stay had been prolonged many days beyond his anticipations, and on the convalescence of the patient he had paid his bill and left for his distant home. Nothing more; he did not even remember that Willard had exchanged with him any other than the most ordinary civilities. After an absence of more than five years business called him once more to the city, and with carpet bag in hand he stood face to face with Willard awaiting his turn to put down his name and to be assigned an apartment. Ere he had uttered a word or given the slightest sign of recognition the traveler was astounded by: How are you, Mr. ———? Hope your boy recovered! Glad to see you again! Show this gentleman to his old room, No. —. The deed was done. The rise in that traveler's self esteem was great, and Willard had added one more to his long line of admirers.

We of to-day have a trite saying "*such a man knows how to keep a hotel.*" It would have applied to Willard in every particular save one—Willard had not a mean hair in his bushy locks.

Chester Jennings was the unseen, but by no means the unimportant partner in the management of the hotel. His quiet duties were to provide supplies and to superintend the details from cellar to garret. He was a tall, slight, serious man, who went about his daily routine apparently as uninterested as a stranger. Both proprietors, fortunately or otherwise, were bachelors, and all the responsibility of engaging and controlling *chambermaids* devolved upon *Mary*, who was known from Maine to Georgia as the efficient *adjutant-general* of Chester Jennings, while the *ancient* Thomas, who locked the front door at midnight, and took supreme command, exercised a restraining supervision over the baggage, boot and fire boys of the establishment. If there was marked disobedience either above or below the culprit was reported to Mr. Jennings, when the simple order "Go to Mr. Willard," was the sentence of dismissal from which there was no appeal. In the dining-room Jennings was commander-in-chief, and the silent clock-work movements of his subordinates might be imitated to advantage in many modern establishments where pompous head waiters strut about in imitation of the guests who were present to meet Mr. Samuel Weller "when he partook of the *soiree* prepared in his honor by the 'Select Footmen of Bath.'"

At what special hour Jennings and Willard held business conferences was a mystery to the earliest riser as well as to the last one who retired when the old porter took formal possession. Certain it was they were in perfect accord, for nothing ever occurred in or about the City Hotel to mar the comfort of its many guests.

CHAPTER SIXTH.

In the immediate vicinity of the City Hotel there still remained some few private residences, though the majority of the buildings had been changed into shops or stores, for at the time there were but few places of business worthy to be designated as warehouses, and they were adjacent to the East River, where all the shipping of the port was moored. Abraham Bininger & Son, the most extensive retail grocers in town, occupied a store on the block above, not far removed from which was the jewelry establishment of Marquand & Co. with an immense gilt eagle over the door, the book store of Edward Long, Milhau's pharmacy, Rushton's drug store, etc. Offices had not become numerous. Lawyers did not at the time constitute a formidable body, while *middle men*, or brokers, as they are now termed, and who have become so numerous in every branch of business or industry, were unknown, for men in their transactions met face to face. Real estate brokers, whose offices are now seen on every thoroughfare, and who are so crowded together on Pine, Cedar, Liberty and Nassau Streets that men marvel by what hidden process so many eke out a subsistence, were represented by only one firm of any note, and even Anthony J. Bleecker & Co.. of No. 5 Broad

Street, would have had but a slim income if all their resources had been derived from commissions on real estate sales. The office of Register, now one of the most lucrative in the peoples' gift, was a *one horse affair*, of little importance. The land speculation of 1835 was the entering wedge for brokers; they then began to thrive on paper projects; imaginary cities were sold and resold for notes payable, but their backs had to be covered with endorsements to ensure the slightest consideration at the banks.

The sanctum of the lawyer had its pine, baize covered table, on which were seen in most admirable disorder, a grey stone ink stand, a plentiful supply of stubby quill pens, a pad of red blotting paper, a boxwood sand box, a meagre scattering of settled cases tied with red tape, pitched here and there, as a cheap mode of advertisement; a few unpainted pine boxes placed one upon the other as a makeshift for a book-case; two or three chairs of divers patterns and degrees of dilapidation; a carpetless floor begrimed with ink and dust. This cheerful abode of legal lore was generally on the second floor back, on some side street, and was dimly lighted by a single window, which had long needed the attention of Aunt Chloe, who did the *chores* and sold apple and cranberry tarts at a penny a piece on the doorstep.

Insurance companies have always been a little "*uppish*" in their ideas. Even in Knickerbocker times the president and directors of the "Non-Combustible" evinced positive aversion to going up stairs. They had a *hankering* for an imposing office, easy of access, where the Board would be proud to meet and partake of crackers and cheese on their all important occasions, when the same set were to be elected over again, always provided they were all alive, and, in case of death, when the survivors could unite as one man in depositing the mantle of responsibility upon the shoulders of the next of kin to the departed co-director. Before insurance companies had grown so *big* or brown stone fronts were in vogue, or elevators were invented, the prominent *equitables* were in the habit of leasing some old family mansion in the business ward, and using the fine roomy parlors with their solid mahogany doors, their high marble mantelpieces, and their imposing brass grates and fenders, for their offices. The desks and railings in the front parlor, the public room, were made of stained pine, but what particular wood the artist had attempted to imitate the artist himself alone could tell. The tint was usually of a reddish hue, and by common consent was called cherry. Conspicuous in the insurance office was the indispensable *iron chest*. This formidable safety contrivance was made of wood covered with straps of sheet iron, crossing each other at right angles and secured by means of immense wrought iron knobs, and in the multiplicity of these unsightly bulges lay its intrinsic value. When duly locked this important affair was considered an impregnable fortress. It would, however, have offered but slight resistance to modern instruments in the hands of men who were impelled to personally inspect the valuables it was supposed to contain. However, in its day it fully answered all the requirements of a lock up, for burglars were few, and they rarely disturbed the slumbers of "*Old Hays*" and his leather capped guardians. *Old Hays!* The name brings vividly to recollection that veteran terror to evil-doers of every grade, sex and age, for even little children would on the instant stop their romping and tearing when grandmother announced the oft-repeated threat, "Old Hays will be after you." Jacob Hays, the father of a family of sons who have for years occupied a prominent position in the financial circles of New York, was high constable and factotum in our criminal court. He was commissioner, superintendent, inspector, captain, sergeant, detective and patrolman combined, and on this individuality the Knickerbocker relied for security to person and property. Old Hays spotted and caught the malefactor, and Dickey Riker, the venerable Recorder, stamped the act as just and proper by consigning the miscreant to prison with simple statement, "*you know you are guilty, and you must suffer some.*"

In those old-fashioned times, if the midnight prowler was apprehended, his doom was certain. The naked law was enforced, the prescribed judgment pronounced, and the sentence carried out to the letter. Perhaps the thieves and their accomplices were poor, but certain it is the modern *Shyster*, with his stay, straw bail, and impertinent sharp practice was not at hand to give the aid of his acquirements in legal lore; but above all, the rabble horde had not attained to that high political position now a sure guarantee against punishment for the most revolting crimes on the calendar. The person of Jacob Hays was most remarkable, and unless he was disguised for some special detective enterprise, his identity was unmistakable. His elongated body and stubby, disproportioned legs were surmounted by a head so large that it almost amounted to a deformity. His features, of the Jewish type, were prominent and striking; his sharp, deep set black eyes were almost hidden by heavy over-hanging eye-brows, which had the effect of imparting a forbidding, sinister aspect to a face which, if analyzed in detail, would have been pronounced intellectually fine. By nature active and shrewd, he was endowed with almost superhuman energy and powers of endurance. His varied exploits of cunning and daring formed one of the topics of the day, they were recited with undisguised wonder, and by passing from mouth to mouth they of course lost none of their chivalric details. The assistants of Old Hays had light duties to perform, and as they were for the most part cartmen who were actively employed during the day, it was not surprising they should now and then take a quiet snooze while playing the extra rôle of watchman at night. Their peaceful slumbers, enjoyed on some slanting cellar door, were seldom disturbed, and then only by some party of youngsters who had put "*too strong a stick*" in their lemonade, and under the influence of this departure were less cautious than usual in the removal of signs and the "wrenching off" of brass knockers as these latter were considered rare trophies as unmistakable evidences of a dare-devil spirit. These desperate breaches of the peace were even overlooked by the kind-hearted, leather-capped cartmen, and it was only when the boys were "real sassy," that they were locked up all night in the watch house, and the next morning led as culprits before the much dreaded "Dickey," who invariably in addition to the small fine imposed, "*to make them suffer some*," scolded them with all the earnest vim of an irate but loving and well-meaning grandmother. Some of these very cartmen who began life as the humble but responsible guardians of slumbering Gotham, by dint of systematic labor and prudent expenditure, were enabled to drop their long brown linen shirts and overalls for a more extended field of usefulness; and not a few of their descendants who inherited the down town homestead with the extra lots attached upon which were built the stalls for horses and cows, now rule with high pretensions, and by their entertainments and costly display of rare exotics have become notables on our most fashionable avenues.

Wall street is Wall street still, so far as its name is concerned. Under Knickerbocker rule it was known as the spot where money changers met, where commerce in its limited ramifications was the theme, and where men of substance found investment for their surplus means. The few banks then needed for deposit and the purposes of legitimate business were there, as was also a small knot of bankers and brokers, who were the innocent forerunners of that busy, restless throng which now surges and seethes, as if the "*day of doom*" had come, and each one had "*to hand in his chips*," when the new Trinity clock strikes three.

The banks had offices fitted up with the simple appointments needed for the transaction of a moderate business. The few clerks employed had abundant yawning time between breakfast and dinner, for they were not furnished with the expensive lunch so indispensable to their gentlemanly successors, who are ensconced behind elaborately wrought black walnut desks, and who can only be distantly gazed at through polished plate glass as they recline on their soft revolving chairs. The paying teller was not so pressed that he had no time to rectify mistakes, but generally found leisure for a friendly chat with his customers. The cashier had a nook of his own, from which he could not only see what was going on, but could also be seen and talked to on business without first obtaining the permission of some stalwart darkey, who now, *Cerberus* like, guards the entrance to that all important personage. Business transactions were then conducted in a slow and cautious manner; men laid their plans ahead, so that the cashier was not unfrequently applied to for the promise of a discount at some still distant day, as the unprovided for indebtedness had begun to prey upon the mind of the applicant, and warning him to make preparations to meet the maturing note. Credit in a great measure supplied the place of capital to the merchant and tradesman, and so long as credit was untarnished, disparity of means was unheeded by money lenders, and the requisite supply could be obtained at the banks without the intervention of middlemen, who now live luxuriously upon commissions extorted from necessitous borrowers. The presidents of these useful banks held their heads deservedly high among their fellow citizens, for the honor was conferred upon men who by their success in business had proven themselves worthy to be the trusted custodians of the property and interests of others. So they were deemed excusable for any little vanity they might display by rapping the pavement rather hard with their gold-headed canes, as they walked with dignified tread through Broadway after their responsibilities had ceased for the day. The salary and emoluments of the position were insignificant, but the distinction conferred by the selection was the grand incentive to its attainment. The banking firms of Prime, Ward & King and Brown Brothers were then almost alone in their calling, as but few individuals came into the market with private European bills of exchange, as the demand would not have warranted the enterprise, and Brown Brothers had gradually grown into this peculiar branch of trade through their extensive dealings with British manufacturers as dry goods commission merchants, in the prosecution of which they had gained the nucleus of their princely fortunes, and formed their world-wide financial connections. The few brokers who congregated in Wall street had desks in basement rooms, which, with but rare exceptions, impressed the passer by with an idea that struggling poverty was the lot of the occupant, who was striving to eke out an existence by the frequent turning of a very small capital, on the plan of Franklin's nimble sixpence. In the windows of two or three of the most prominent of these basements were to be seen packages of the bills of country banks, then designated as uncurrent money, from the fact that they were not receivable at par over the counters of our city institutions, though they were considered a perfect legal tender in trade by retail dealers in payment for family supplies. This wild cat money was procured by the brokers at a stipulated rate of discount, and resold by them at a slight advance to mechanics and manufacturers, who in turn purchased it and paid it out at par to their employees. Small stacks of foreign and domestic coin lay side by side with these paper tokens, and these jointly represented the stock in trade; in other words, the window sill held the entire capital of the concern. Over the entrance, "Exchange Office" was posted, and a minute tin slab stuck in one corner of the window announced to the public the name of the proprietor.

Transactions in securities were few and insignificant in amount, mainly for investment. The greed for speculation had not tainted the plodding habits of business men, wrapt up as they were in their peculiar calling, satisfied with limited credit and contented with moderate gains. The railway and mining mania was unborn. The stocks and mortgage bonds, which now form the staple of the gigantic operations which daily, nay hourly, make and unmake scores of desperate speculators, were not in existence; they had not drawn into the seething cauldron of Wall Street wealth from every corner of the civilized globe. When to these countless millions was added our inflated currency at the opening of the rebellion, the spirit of speculation pervaded all classes. Men became mad in their unnatural desire of becoming suddenly rich, and Wall Street became the magnet of attention. Men of all ages and conditions, leaving homes and former avocations, flocked thither, confident of realizing in a brief period a fortune, which in the slow route of trade would consume a lifetime. "Brains, not labor," was the motto emblazoned on the banner of the day. The more unscrupulous the operator, the more assured seemed the success. Honor, honesty, self-esteem—all the higher qualities which should attach to mankind were thrown aside in this wild chase after gain. Up to this period a comparatively small number of brokers earned a fair subsistence by executing commissions at the Stock Exchange. The community at large, and even the denizens of the city, thought little and cared less whether the bulls or bears were in the ascendant, as the daily transactions at the Board were of so limited a nature as to have no effect on the general money market. Thousands of well-to-do men lived and died without even puzzling their brains about the ups and downs of the stock list. The great change came, as it were, "*in the twinkling of an eye.*" From early morn till dark the street devoted to stock transactions was filled with an excited crowd of the new found worshippers of Mammon. Old brokers were overwhelmed with commissions, new ones by hundreds rushed to the scene of excitement, and soon found ample employment in the increasing demand for their services. The din of voices could not drown the babel of tongues, for all the nationalities of the globe seemed to be represented in the surging throng. The shrewd Israelite, the cunning Yankee, the philosophic German, the mercurial Frenchman, the dignified Spaniard, the indolent Italian, the phlegmatic John Bull, even the spectacled blue stocking was present. Millions had become the goal. Dollars, numbered by thousands only, were too insignificant to arrest attention. Supplies of stock were quickly furnished to satisfy the greedy man of speculation; schemes equal in variety to the famed South Sea Bubble were promptly matured. Mines of gold, silver, copper, even of humble lead were opportunely discovered. Oil spurted up in every ravine and floated on every creek. New railroads were surveyed, organized, built only in imagination, and were represented by stock, which was sold and resold before the printer's ink became dry, which was the only certificate of their value. Fools wondered, thinking men pondered, yet all plunged into this whirling torrent of reckless gambling. The mechanic, the artizan, even the methodical bookkeeper was infected with the contagion, and roused to desperate deeds of venture, as bending over his humdrum ledger thus reasoning to himself, "No one can wonder that I, an humble bookkeeper, eking out a bare existence on a salary which is daily lessening in intrinsic value, should be lured by such a prospect of competency; many a lucky acquaintance has twitted me about my timidity and laughed at my fears. Even this I could have withstood, but the fact stares me in the face, that *gold* is two hundred; in other words, my paper dollar received as salary is becoming daily of less value, and my employer is apparently so obtuse as not to perceive that it is impossible for me to exist on a representation of money so nearly approaching to rags. I will venture my small savings as margin in Wall Street, and become a man among men. What should I buy? whose advice shall I seek? were my cogitations as I hastened to add my little self and my small capital to the wild confusion that reigned in and about the Stock Exchange. My destination was soon reached, but for awhile I forgot my errand, forgot myself. 'An eighth'—'a quarter' —'three eights'—'buyer three'—'seller three' —'regular'—'cash'—'take it'—'sold'—'broker up,' these and other equally cabalistic terms were bellowed from lungs which would have drowned the frantic yells of a Sixth Ward fire company during a most exciting race."

"The crowd was dense, I tried to push through, I tried to back out, and was at last compelled to follow in the wake of a practiced *habitué*, who doubtless having money to borrow or contract to complete, was elbowing a passage through the serried ranks. When on the point of giving up in despair, I chanced to meet an acquaintance; was introduced to his broker, deposited my hard-earned margin, and by his advice bought "one hundred Erie." The important end was accomplished, I was interested in stocks; on the high-road to fortune, and no longer a subject for the jokes of my associates. In that one moment I had forever, as I thought, discarded drudgery and "make or break" had become my motto. I hastened back to the counting-house and with an assumed composure stood once more face to face with my duty. Dull work was the ledger on that day; one hundred Erie appeared at every footing, and stocks were everywhere about me as I nervously waited for the hour of freedom to come that I might hasten to learn the result of my venture. The time at length rolled by, and I found myself unconsciously on a dead run, in company with hundreds of others who were impelled by the same mad impulse. "Market strong. Erie up one per cent.," was the reply to my anxious inquiry. One hundred dollars, a whole month's salary, made in a few short hours. To-morrow may double, triple, perhaps quadruple that. Fortune lighted up my future. Man naturally seeks congenial companionship. After a hearty meal I almost flew to the Fifth Avenue Hotel, then the night rendezvous of the restless spirits who knew no day, no night, no rest in their pursuit of lucre, and who each evening transferred to that famed hotel their bewildering traffic, leaving Wall Street for the time to rest in solitary gloom. Here the busy telegraph was continuously at work, adding fuel to the fire. Battles lost or won; recognition by England or France; McClellen flanked, etc., were circulated "thick and fast, like lightning from the Summer cloud," by Bull or Bear as interest dictated. To me this manœuvreing was a sealed book in all else save when Erie was the immediate interest. It had already become a part of my being; was mingled with my brandy; it added to the solace of my segar, as after midnight I dragged myself wearily homeward to my couch, on which I threw myself with

Care for my bedfellow, and passed the night with conflicting rumors pictured in my dreams. Morning dawned and I dreaded the suspense which awaited me during business hours. I dared not relinquish my situation so was compelled to perform my duties with my accustomed regularity; but above all must be careful to give no clue by which my employers could possibly suspect me of having embarked in speculation, against which they had so repeatedly and so earnestly warned me. During the day I had opportunities to hear reports of my darling Erie, and great was my dread lest I should betray my unbounded joy when the announcement was casually made that Erie had *"gone up"* five per cent. "Five hundred dollars ahead," it was almost too much for my poor crazy brain to withstand, without giving vent to my enthusiasm. On my release from the day's thraldom, the glad tidings were confirmed by my broker. Better sell and realize was the monition of my timid, untutored judgment. The market is strong, says the Stock List. "Anything is a purchase," is shouted by the crowd of knowing ones and eager buyers cry their bids, and snatch up each offered lot. I'll wait. What is my judgment worth when compared with those of men who make stocks their study, and besides my banker assures me he will watch my Erie as if it was his own. I decided to wait at any rate until to-morrow. To-morrow came and passed; a whole week elapsed and the market was still buoyant; the Bulls were jubilant, I being one of the named fraternity was in ecstacies of delight; my margin was more than dollars—a whole years' salary acquired in one short week. But with all my delight I was worn with continuous anxiety. I had become one of the restless, sleepless throng. Erie and I were one; all else an uninteresting blank, and I firmly resolved to sever the connection, to part with my idol. Nay, in my excitement vowed I would sell it, even though Wall Street jeer and tauntingly reproach me for my folly. Fortified by this resolution, I calmly presented myself within the Broker's Sanctum armed with a written order to sell at market prices. The room was full; clerks were driving like madmen to compare the business of the hour. Orders to buy were pouring in from all sides, among which my Erie was prominently named. Why should I sell that which so many are anxious to buy? Like a flash my determination has altered and I mingled with the buzzing crowd that I might hear the flying rumors of the hour. The leading Bear of the street was largely short of Erie:—tomorrow his contracts mature—he cannot borrow the stock he will need—he will be compelled to buy it in the open market—Erie must go up twenty per cent. before his wants are supplied—such was the story I gleaned from *Reliable Information*. I did not then know the false-hearted jade, so tore up my order to sell and excitedly walked home, with a small fortune which I should clutch on the morrow, when this short operator would be obliged to pay me a fabulous profit on my speculation. Another dreamy night, "that bright dream was his last," my last, I should say, for that eventful morning revealed to me one of the pit-falls which Reliable Information digs to engulf the unfortunate possessors of small margins who venture on the quick sands of Wall Street. The knowing ones, who, like myself, had been posted as to the events of the day, were early on hand to take advantage of the most opportune moment in order to realize the highest figures. The Erie which had been previously loaned to the great Bear was duly called in; and to the great surprise of the young Bulls was promptly delivered; his contracts all punctually met, but no stock had been bought. Soon as the shrewd game had been fully played, the street was flooded with stock. Mortgage Bonds had been quietly bought up and privately converted, and the confident Bulls found themselves loaded with a burthen too weighty to carry. The panic spread as one after another made frantic efforts to unload; "*Sauve qui peut*" soon became the order for getting out of Erie. I fortunately got out, but that was all, for my little margin with its accrued earnings were swallowed up in the whirlpool. I got out a wiser man, at least in this, and I would have my limited experience engraved on the minds of everyone who dares to venture on untried speculation. To such I would say, "Always sell when you have a profit, be it ever so small, and do not permit Reliable Information to induce you to wait until to-morrow. Capital makes information to suit its own ends, and sells it to such as dare speculate on small hard-earned margins." The bookkeeper's experience has been the lot of thousands, who, like him, were led astray by the fatal mirage and engulfed in irretrievable ruin. But let us leave this sad digression and return to the peaceful Knickerbocker Wall Street, where hours of consultation and "considering" were required before a share of stock was purchased.

Lotteries were then legal enterprises, and the Exchange Office men were enabled to turn an honest penny by slyly furnishing checks to their customers. This petty species of gambling, though approved by the Legislature, was looked upon with distrust by the stiff necked majority, and those who betrayed the weakness of habitually trying their luck, had the boldness to face the music and openly purchase their selected combinations, though there was not the stigma attached which now compels the infatuated devotee of magic numbers to slink behind screens and to carefully conceal his illicit purchase from the lynx-eyed guardians of public morals.

Aaron Clark, a most popular and highly respected Mayor of the city, was extensively engaged in this business, and his name and occupation were placed over his office door on the conspicuous south-west corner of Broadway and Park Place. Mr. Clark had many intimate friends among the stanchest *pillars*, with whom he was often seen in earnest consultation, and naughty little boys would sometimes tell "how they had picked up queer pieces of paper which Grandpa had accidentally dropped," and on returning the same had been quietly rewarded with a bright penny.

CHAPTER SEVENTH.

The old Tontine Society, though still nominally in existence, is rapidly approaching its final dissolution, and is one of the last links which bind the present with the past Knickerbocker days. This venerable association began in what will soon become a misty era. It was founded by a company of merchants, and was incorporated by special act of Legislature near the close of the last century. Two hundred and three shares were subscribed for, at two hundred dollars each. With the proceeds, the lot on the northwest corner of Wall and Water streets was purchased, and upon it the Original Coffee House was erected. According to the first clause in the articles of incorporation it was to be used and kept as a coffee house, and for no other use and purpose whatsoever, until the number of corporators should be, by death, reduced to seven; at which period the property was to be divided among the survivors in fee simple, and the trust to cease. The coffee house proper has long since disappeared. Many years ago a change was effected in the original agreement, the building altered and leased for mercantile purposes, and the rents divided among the survivors in interest. There are but few now remaining among us who can remember when the Tontine Coffee House was a central landmark:

but few who were present, when their grandfathers convened within its walls to indulge in moderate conviviality and to talk over the religious, political and commercial topics of the times. These worthies were not myths; they carried into outdoor life the same dignified bearing, which insured them the unqualified respect of their individual families, and they exacted from their juniors the defference they claimed as the prerogative of gray hairs. They constituted themselves a committee of general supervision; in matters of serious import their decisions were received as law, and public opinion was to a great extent based upon their approval. An old writer of eminence at the time, says: "Their conclusions were universally respected." In proof of which he instances their successful protest against a fashion of the period which was considered burthensome to the poor but respectable class of the community. "At the time it was the arbitrary custom to distribute indiscriminately expensive linen scarfs at all funerals, and many poor but worthy people were sorely pinched to provide this apparently necessary mark of respect for deceased relatives. Some prominent members of the Tontine Society called a meeting at the Coffee House to discuss this subject, at which nearly two hundred of those whose weight of character gave force to their decision, signed a pledge that they would abstain from the custom of supplying scarfs except to the dominie and the attending physician. Their prompt, decided action proved the death knell to this useless, oppressive fashion." But in matters of more vital import, when really great public interests were at stake, a voice has gone forth from the old Coffee House which was listened to, and the words of warning or counsel heeded throughout the length and breadth of the land. The final close of the Tontine Association must be near at hand, when the story of its life will be written and the ramifications of its influence made public. Its records which spread over three-quarters of a century will form a most important social and commercial chapter in the history of New York. They should embrace the sayings and doings of many of the best and wisest men of their generation, whom the people delighted to honor, and whose memories will be cherished when their strong, shining qualities are gleaned from an authentic source.

All the banks, insurance offices, with bankers and brokers even included, occupied but a very limited portion of Wall street; indeed, most of them could find ample accommodation in one of the modern edifices which now line that crowded thoroughfare. Some private families still clung to their old-time houses, loth to tear themselves away from surroundings associated with the most tender ties; but by far the larger majority of the homesteads had been converted into shops, as the rents, which could be obtained for business purposes, were deemed too extravagant for a mere domicile. Three or four hundred dollars would hire a first-class residence up in Dey or Fulton streets, while a hundred or two more added, landed the rising family in the aristocratic Park Place, among the Motts, Hones, Carters, Haggerties, Austins, Beekmans and Hosacks of the period.

The Wall Street Presbyterian Church, presided over by Dr. Phillips, stood on the north side, between Nassau street and Broadway, and held its own until it was ("a Sabbath day journey") removed from the majority of its communicants, when the property was sold at a high figure—say one-twentieth of the sum which would now be considered a bargain, and the dominie with his flock found refuge in the stone edifice on the corner of Fifth avenue and Eleventh street, on the very outskirts of the fashionable boundary. Even there it is no longer safe, the Goths and Vandals of speculation are intrenching it on all sides, and it must soon give place to the hum of business or the din of revelry.

In close proximity to the old church, two men, whose names have since become famous, laid the foundation of a peculiar enterprise which has expanded into a wealthy and powerful corporation, whose stocks are daily quoted and watched on the Street. Harnden and Adams both started singly and alone with but small capital, but each possessed indomitable will and was imbued with determined perseverance. In the beginning, for a considerable time, each was his own and only messenger, and a couple of carpet bags sufficed for the stowage of the express packages entrusted to their care. Boston in one direction and Philadelphia in the other was the terminus of the route traversed, and three departures per week amply served the requirements of trade. So quiet was the start of this now over-shadowing monopoly that it was not until a wagon or two was brought into requisition, which were lettered either as Adams' or Harnden's Express, that the majority of citizens were aware of its existence. The unparalleled success of this branch of industry is attributable to the strict honesty and undeviating promptness which characterized its outset, and to these are the present stockholders indebted for the vast patronage they now enjoy. Among the early employees of the Adams Express was a busy, lively lad, who was determined to make a living. He cried papers on the streets when that was a very precarious undertaking, but was ever ready to hold a horse or run an errand to earn a small gratuity. By some fortuitous circumstance this boy drifted under the quick eye of Adams, and upon due trial, he proving to be both trustworthy and bright, became a fixture in the business. He grew with its growth and his mind kept pace and expanded with all the ramifications of its ever outstretching branches, and at a ripe middle age John Hoey is the competent, responsible and respected superintendent of the great Adams Express, with which he has been associated without interruption from its inception and his earliest boyhood.

Each of the corners of Wall street, formed by its intersection with Broadway, was occupied as a fashionable tailor shop, the firms being Howard, Keeler & Scofield and St. John & Toucey. Each had an extensive trade, both in and out of the city, founded upon the belief that the garments they furnished were *everlasting;* a great recommendation at a period when the fashions were not fickle, and a great coat or Spanish cloak was considered *"good for best"* during fifty Winters and could then be cut up for common wear. Solid West of England cloths were in vogue, and tradition says, was so finely sewn and finished that it required hours of labor and a sharp knife to remove the nap from a single square inch. One of these "*time-defiers*" of a snuff brown shade, was seen last Winter on Broadway protecting a wealthy veteran of four score from the chilling blasts. On hasty inspection no shade of giving way was perceptible; but there it was a monument of the past. Its angular back, straight, narrow sleeves, scant, stiff, rolling collar and lappel, long flowing tails, bearing unimpeachable testimony that it was no modern fraud, but was the genuine handwork of the veteran Howard, who long years since at a ripe old age ceased cutting both coats and capes.

On the East side of Broadway, just South of Wall Street, there was a busy little crib on the ground-floor. Its windows were ornamented with geraniums and a number of cages whose imprisoned inmates made the neighborhood cheerful with their melody. It was a barber shop; nothing more, nothing less. Custom in those days decided that the Fathers should shave themselves, verily no slight undertaking, for few allowed their whiskers to grow, and a moustache, to say the least, was damaging to credit; the dare-devil who had the audacity to sport one was surely denounced as an adventurer, and homebred youth were warned to avoid his acquaintance. Most of the "ancients" wore their hair short at the top and powdered it freely, allowing their back hair to grow long, when it was stiffly braided.

This appendage was elegantly styled a pig-tail, a liberal rendering doubtless of the French *"queue."* This ornament necessitated the employment of skilled labor for its proper adjustment. So the barber was patronized by the dignified patricians. The barber has been a privileged and courted character since the dawn of civilization; privileged to chatter, and courted for what in other men would be set down as too impertinent for endurance, and, strange to relate, patronized by old and young in proportion to his glibness of speech and fertility of imagination. The Dutchman is conceded to be the most silent and phlegmatic specimen of our race, *poor Lo* not excepted; but let one of these taciturn Teutons adopt the trade of "shaver," and no sooner has he placed a man's head in position, wrapped the victim in a damp towel, slushed his face with suds, and stropped the razor on the palm of his hand, than away goes his unruly member, popping off questions, opinions, and declarations with a vim that would excite the French nation almost to the verge of revolution. The barber, as a rule, does not read the papers, for they are too slow and by far too circumscribed in detail to furnish the supply of entertainment needed by a tip-top tonsorial artist; he is therefore compelled to vigorously "pump" certain customers that he may administer to some other the soothing strains of enchanting scandal, and thus enable them to survive the scraping ordeal. Maniort, the proprietor of *The* Knickerbocker Barber Shop, seemed specially created for his peculiar calling; a polite, garrulous Frenchman, and *"par excellence"* the most accomplished gossip in town. No modern extra *Herald* could beat him in gaining possession of the newest rumor, and it would take the most determined set of newsboys to disseminate it as expeditiously as he effected it through the various channels he had at command. The most minute "*faux pas*" affecting the male or female; even the slightest suspicion of a surmise that came into his net, was served that evening at every tea-table of note in Gotham, and at a moderate cost —six and a quarter cents, with a clean shave thrown in gratis. Rumor has it that Louis Napoleon and the jolly French barber were on peculiar intimate terms while the former was a sojourner here; whether true or false, certain it is that when the Emperor was firmly established on his throne the mercurial scandal-monger folded his tent and flew away to the Gay Capital, where he had a more enlarged field and a grander patron for his unsurpassed talent.

Directly opposite the barber shop, on the corner of Rector Street, and overshadowed by imposing Trinity, stood the original Grace Church, then as now the chosen shrine of the "*crème de la crème*," among that portion of society who especially affect the imposing ritual of Episcopacy. Doctor Wainwright was for many years its beloved pastor, than whom a more respected, genial, Christian gentleman never entered a New York pulpit. To attend service at Grace was eminently fashionable, although there were other places of worship in the city, whose congregations could boast of an equal amount of wealth and beauty. Still, both young men and women fancied there was an air of quiet gentility in and about it not to be met with elsewhere. The worthy rector was a passionate lover of music, and prided himself not a little on his judgment of the divine art and on the nicety of his criticism. As would most naturally follow in the wake of a taste so decided, the impressive chants were given at Grace in a perfected style not equalled by any choir in the city, which, of course, had the effect of attracting many to its portals on each succeeding Sabbath, who by virtue of baptismal rites were looked upon as backsliders from the original fold into which they had been unconsciously borne in puling infancy. This state of affairs gave rise to no inconsiderable amount of comment, and some sore heart-burnings on the part of zealous Reformed Dutch parents and friends who still clung to the monstrous nasal psalmody, to endure which had become a part and parcel of their existence. Miss Emma Gillingham was the leading lady of the efficient choir, whose rich tones had been cultivated by Sconcia; and she was not infrequently assisted by Charles E. Horn and Austin Phillips, two of the sweetest singers New York has ever heard. The aid afforded by these cultivated songsters was a powerful adjunct to the Doctor's polished efforts for the spread of Christianity, and Grace Church was always filled to its utmost capacity, while wealthy, pretentious Trinity, "the mother of us all," who in these feverish, exciting times still each day tries to soothe Wall Street with her mellow chimes, could fitly be compared to "a banquet hall deserted." It certainly was the unseen and spiritual which attracted, for the exterior of Old Grace presented nothing to command attention even from "the stranger within our gates." A plain, square brick structure, with no turret, no steeple, not even the usual cross to designate its particular denomination, or to distinguish it from an overgrown school house. At some period it had probably been painted white; but long exposure had imparted to its walls a dingy yellow tinge that was far from being agreeable to the eye. Nevertheless it was *the* church, and "I have attended Grace this morning," could not be uttered with a more satisfied air by a modern belle tricked out in all the furbelows of 1871, than the same sentence was spoken hundreds of times from beneath bonnets one of which would make headgear for the whole congregation of New Grace, if the gew-gaws with which they are ornamented could by any means be dispensed with.

Few of the thousands who daily pass in and out of our dilapidated crazy post-office* stop to give one thought as to the past history of the venerable pile now so rapidly approaching its final demolition. None have the leisure to make the enquiry, but should some stray visitor chance to pause and for a moment wonder for what special use it had originally been planned, he would have to tarry long before encountering one in the eager expectant throng of applicants for letters who could give him a satisfactory reply to his queries.

The Middle Dutch Church, now the Post Office,

---
* It must be borne in mind that this was written in 1871.

was one of the oldest and most noted places of worship on Manhattan Island. For some years prior to its transfer to the Government the associate ministers in charge were Drs. Brownlee, Knox and De Witt. The latter alone remains of a trio like whom, all things considered, will never again be convened in this city. This old building was the last gathering place of a class who represented the past in its hard strict simplicity of worship, and was the connecting link between the old and new school in everything, religion not excepted. The masses in our midst have not the most remote idea of its quaint interior in former days. The entrance was from Cedar Street, and the pulpit occupied that end of the building; that is, the entire space between the two doors of admission. This pulpit, so far as dimensions are concerned, would answer the purpose of a modern reception room. It was reached from either side by a flight of at least a dozen carpeted steps, ornamented by massive mahogany balusters. At the top of these stairs there was a door through which the Dominie entered; when that was closed after him, and the good man seated, he was most effectually hidden from mortal eyes.

Over this pulpit was suspended what was called a sounding-board, a contrivance doubtless intended to reverberate and re-echo the terrors of the law. A large square velvet cushion ornamented at each corner with heavy pendant tassels was the resting-place for the Bible. The pews were not modelled for ease, their straight, high backs and narrow seats were the ideal of discomfort; a lounging posture was an impossibility; when mounted on the seat no one but a long-limbed man could touch the floor; so the sufferings of women and children can be imagined. Bolt upright, eyes forward and limbs dangling was the order when once ensconced and the pew-door closed. Grandmother had a high cushion for her feet in warm weather, and a box made of wood and sheet iron, which contained live hickory coals, denominated a foot-stove, for winter, so the dear old lady was as comfortable as circumstances would permit. We youngsters were often wicked enough to envy her these luxuries, and not infrequently had arguments with Betty with regard to this partiality, but were soon abashed by the firm declaration "that if we didn't stop talkin' so wicked the b'ars would ketch us sure," for, next to grandmother, Betty was authority in all spiritual as well as secular matters. On either side of the pulpit, in special pews, sat the elders and deacons, six of each order, with their assigned position so arranged that the whole congregation was under inspection. To the youthful, irreligious, unsophisticated attendant, these twelve men seemed the incarnation of cold relentless piety divested of every human frailty. Of divers names, sizes, avocations, degrees of intelligence, they appeared as they sat in their accustomed places to become as one man. When one rose they all stood up; when one sat down all followed suit, as if acted upon simultaneously by an electric wire. Their black dress coats seemed to have been made by the same tailor; their white neck cloths cut from one piece of cambric, washed, ironed and folded by the same laundress; the bow knots even appeared to have been adjusted by the same hand, while the same unearthly pallor and fixed expression characterized the faces of the twelve. When at length the minister rose, consulted his watch, placed his handkerchief under one side of the Bible, and had slyly slipped his notes from under his gown on to the Bible, the sermon began. Then came, at least in one sense, a positive relief. The twenty-four eyes of the twelve elders and deacons were raised as if by word of command, and for an hour at least were fixed seemingly without winking upon the Dominie as he expounded his version of the Law. That protracted harangue afforded the opportunity to scan these greatly-feared twelve with no probable risk of meeting one of their cold fixed eyes. No ray of soul light could be detected on their countenances; not even when the minister became so warmly eloquent as to cause woman's cheek to glow with sympathetic excitement. The torments of the bottomless pit proclaimed by the uncompromising Brownlee; the beatitude of the blest hopefully dwelt on by the gentle Knox; the pressing invitation to repentance heralded in powerful tones by the more youthful and impulsive De Witt, were alike unavailing to produce the slightest variation in the stereotyped countenances of these twelve leading dignitaries of the Middle Dutch Church. They sat as motionless as statues, rendered rigid by their sense of duty; the top line of a copybook was not more exact in its crosses and dots.

Still, incomprehensible as it may seem, they were men, and gentle ones at that. Once out of their pews they mingled cheerfully with their fellows in social life; grasped a brother's hand with a warm pressure, and their purse-strings were not tightly drawn when charity called for her tithes.

If these indelible recollections should chance to meet the eye of any who in youth were led by their parents "like lambs to the slaughter" twice at least on each Sunday, to attend divine service at the Old Church, they cannot fail to recall the unspeakable feeling of relief they experienced when the stated exercises were ended, the joy with which they sprang to their feet to give ease to their almost paralyzed limbs, but above all, the happy relaxation of the mind when convinced that the terrible ordeal was passed.

Another striking feature in the routine of service, which happily has passed away with the other stern realities of the times was the singing at the Middle Dutch, for that formed no inconsiderable portion of the strain inflicted upon youthful nerves. The Middle Dutch had no organ, not that the congregation was too poor to indulge in such a luxury, for in truth it had the means at command to purchase, and pile tier upon tier the most costly ones Europe could furnish, but the appliance was registered by common consent as an invention of the arch enemy to distract mortals from the real essence of praise. In the vacant space under the elevated pulpit was placed a solitary chair, in front of which stood an ordinary table, upon which were ranged side by side a hymn-book, a devotional Psalmody, and a tuning fork—a small steel instrument used to pitch the desired key. This space was the exclusive domain of the chorister. The chorister of the Middle Dutch was a severely taxed functionary, as he was compelled to stand three times during each service facing the gaze of the entire congregation, and maintain a calm, stoical expression, which would have qualified him for the exalted position of elder, had he not been compelled from the peculiar duties of his station to make some contortions of visage, so the matter of eldership was set at rest. Being the leader it was not in accordance with the dignity of his profession to permit the wondrous organ of sound with which Nature had gifted him to be overpowered, or his personality to be for a single moment lost in the din created by a thousand enthusiastic warblers, each one of whom was straining every nerve with the determination to be heard at least on earth. Twelve stanzas and a doxology must have been a fearful tax even upon a man of his well tested organs of respiration. For years he held this post of danger, apparently uninjured, defying alike bronchitis and consumption, for when grown gray at his post there was no apparent diminution of power or endurance. If Chorister Earl be still living, (and there is no valid reason for the "taking off" of this iron-clad specimen of the race,) it was a marvel that he was not engaged to lead that concourse of sweet sounds, which, a short time since, shook the foundation of Bunker Hill, and yet vibrate in the ears of the delighted Boston critics. Gilmore must be young and untraveled not to have heard of Chorister Earl. Dominie, elders, deacons, chorister, tuning-fork and all, have passed under the swath of the "Scythe Bearer," and their descendants are carefully nestling in a white marble structure of exquisite finish and beauty on the corner of Fifth Avenue and Twenty-Ninth Street, surrounded by fashion and worldly pomp. In the modern Middle Dutch, smiling clergymen delight their listeners with short, well constructed, moral essays; smart, dapper elders and deacons, with beaming countenances, gay neckties and jewelled shirt fronts, are the admiration of the young. No chorister and tuning-fork, but in their stead a charming *Prima Doña*, sustained by a Tenoré and Basso of acknowledged operatic reputation, is hidden from public gaze by the rich curtains of the organ loft, whence she warbles with exquisite skill the choicest solos of modern art, while the new school reclines on velvet couches so enchanted by the performance that were it not for some vague, misty associations connected with the day and place, it would be acknowledged by the clapping of jewelled hands and a floral tribute.

It is not very long ago, but since the epoch when modern improvements displaced the rigid formalities of the Dutch Church service, that a meeting for some specified object of religious interest was held on a Sunday evening in one of the most fashionable of our Presbyterian churches, celebrated not only for the eloquence of its pastor but for the brilliancy of its choir. Ministers of all denominations were invited to be present and participate in the exercises. Prominent among the clergy who were seated in the pulpit was a venerable divine, whose massive presence brought back the past with vivid minuteness; age had dealt leniently with his imposing, Websterian outline, and his undimmed, sympathetic eye, demonstrated the deep interest he felt. He, however, took no active part until near the close, when, by request of the pastor, he rose to his feet, and spreading out his arms as if to include all in his heartfelt invitation, he enunciated in a deep, rich voice, that rang through the frescoed arches of the church, "Let us rise, and conclude this service of God, by singing to His praise the five hundred and sixty-second hymn,—'Hark! the Song of Jubilee.'" The almost inspired lay of Montgomery was felt and understood, as it was powerfully declaimed by that master mind. The effect of the appeal was electrical; the peals of the organ were swallowed by that sounding song of praise. The old Knickerbocker leaven had for the moment forced its way through the thin covering of fashionable conventionality.

The old Middle Dutch bell still clangs as of yore; not, however, to call sinners to repent and shun the fire of the hereafter, but to summon the firemen of our city to do their secular duty in quelling some present and visible conflagration.

In the immediate vicinity of the old church there lived a man, who was a well-known, eccentric character, but respected as a good and useful citizen. Grant Thorburn, the florist, might be termed an extraordinary genius, with a personal identity seldom encountered in the common walks of life. His shuffling gait, the result of a malformation, made him always conspicuous

even in a crowded thoroughfare, while his strict
Quaker garb, of which sect he was a member,
added to the grotesque outline of his short, unprepossessing figure. Grant was continually on
the street, bowing right and left to every one he
chanced to meet; but whether this peculiarity
was the result of nervous sensibility, or as some
asserted, in a conceited idea of his own importance, matters little. He was a harmless busybody, and occupied much of his time by writing
letters to the press expressive of his views on any
special topic which was at the time uppermost in
public attention. Some of these literary effusions
afforded much amusement, as his sentiments
were always expressed in unmeasured terms, but
in the main were only on a par with similar displays of erratic minds who aim at achieving some
kind of notoriety. Grant's individual business
always appeared to be of secondary consideration
with him. At any hour of the day he found
leisure for a protracted chat, and was ever
ready to listen to and frequently did embark
heart and soul in the doubtful schemes of petty
speculation which were then started with limited
public support. But little by little they gained
ground against the ruling prejudice of the day,
until at length the "Mulberry Mania" became
epidemic, and for a considerable time was the
engrossing topic not only in the city but for
miles around. Pamphlets were circulated, detailing in figures that were never known to lie,
the enormous profits which were sure to be the
result of the intelligent culture of the "*Morus
Multicaulis.*" Editorials on the fecundity of the

silk worm were daily spun out in the blanket sheets; farms, garden and city lots even, were transformed into nurseries. Shining silk was not yet, but was soon to be the universal covering. Poor but serviceable cotton was spurned as the "makeshift" of a dark age, and the whole Knickerbocker tribe was at an early day to be arrayed in brocade. The contagion spread with such rapidity that hundreds of the old school, well-to-do, plodding men, abandoned their lifelong avocations and invested every dollar they could rake and scrape, and even when that did not suffice, pledged their credit to its utmost tension to secure controlling interest in this bubble. After creating a somewhat protracted excitement this expensive "hobby horse" was ridden to death. A few sharpers quietly sold out and withdrew when the precious trees were selling at a penny per leaf, disposing of their interest to saving men, who, in turn, were soon too glad to accept the price of fire-wood for their bargains, when by the sudden reaction they found themselves involved in pecuniary ruin. Grant Thorburn, as will be surmised, was one of the first to embark in an enterprise, which from his occupation of agriculturalist he would be supposed to comprehend. He entered largely into the work; he planted widely on Long Island, and with his inflammable temperament jumped in imagination from the silk-worm to the loom; to the full stocked warehouse; to fortune; but only to find himself so hampered by bills payable as forever after to cripple his independence and materially to lessen his self-love. Grant lived to a ripe old age sustained by a pittance in the Custom House. He wrote occassionally for the press, but the nature of his manifestoes was changed from the decided dictation and self-assertion so characteristic of his earlier efforts.

CHAPTER EIGHTH.

Eating-houses, now more politely termed restaurants, were limited in number, commonplace in appointments, and would not ordinarily be deemed of sufficient importance to warrant even a passing notice. But as they were the creations, so to speak, of a foreign element in the city, they may be alluded to collectively as one of the stepping-stones which cropped out as by degrees, primitive Gotham gave way to Metropolitan New York. They were established in the business portion of the city, and their patronage was derived from the necessities they afforded, and not, as is the case at present, from their gastronomical luxuries. Dinner was the meal upon which they depended, and the noon hour their harvest time. The clatter of dishes, the bustle of the hurrying waiters, the steam from the savory compounds were perhaps appurtenants to such a place, as a matter, but, as there ever was need for a novice in such matters before he could enjoy a repast served in one of many beer refreshment saloons. The curious in such affairs can have ocular, oral and nasal experience by simply visiting one of the cellars now in full blast under Fulton Market. High noon is the precise time to see the cauldron bubble. The scene then to be witnessed on any week day is a counterpart of the earliest efforts of New York purveyors. Evening, or more properly, night customers were to most of them unknown. The one or two noted exceptions will be named hereafter. Saloons were not the mode with gentlemen, and women would have endured the gnawings of hunger before venturing to enter the most retired one on the list. As late as 1835 James Thompson, a confectioner, opened a store at 171 Broadway, for the sale of cakes and other dainties, to accommodate ladies who were engaged in shopping; but for a long time this embryo Delmonico languished in neglect, even though the sisters of the proprietor, middle-aged women, were the sole attendants, and it was situated on the most frequented portion of the promenade. Tempting *morceaux* were displayed in the windows, but all in vain, sideway glances were the only recognition vouchsafed them by dame or miss; society ruled that it was not proper to enter and partake; so the grandmothers and mothers of the present generation trudged home content. It has been the rule for society to enact laws for its own government. Whether the Knickerbocker law, which has been superseded as being too stringent, was right or not will be fully demonstrated when the coming generation reviews the conduct of their maternal ancestors. "All's well that ends well" is a truism to be duly considered by any class of society. Modesty, under old-fashioned rule, signified diffidence, purity, truth; it shrank from public gaze, it moved in a quiet, unostentatious manner, and selected the humble but beautiful violet as its emblem. Its possessor was surrounded by unmistakable evidences of its real presence; the delicate mantling of the cheek, the half-closed eyelid, the slightly stooping position, the noiseless, sliding step, the subdued tone could not be counterfeited by the most cunning art of the coquette. Man recognized it at a glance, and was ready "to avenge even a look that threatened it with insult." Chivalry is not dead, although the fact has been asserted with burning eloquence; it has merely fallen into a condition of lethargy, as the primary object of its inspiration has assumed, under modern rule, to be her own champion, guide and protector. Woman, old and young, sick and poor, beautiful or hideous, has chosen the responsibility of standing alone; she has clipped one by one the clinging tendrils of her nature, and with head erect and defiant step resolved to battle against the world. The finale of this new departure has been depicted in the past; history will once more repeat itself.

The dining-room of Clark & Brown, one of the most extensive, was on Maiden Lane, near to its junction with Liberty street. It was the resort of such who particularly delighted in roast beef very *rare* and cut in thick slices, or a beefsteak scarcely warmed through, English plum-pudding and a mug of the best "half and half" in the city, brewed at Poughkeepsie or Philadelphia, but just for the name of the thing, "you know," called Burton Stock Ale. The peculiar mode of serving meats and the strong, black London Dock brandy did not meet the approval of the uneducated Knickerbocker stock, who had been reared on thoroughly cooked food, and preferred made gravies to the pure red juice, so prominent an article in the John Bull creed. So the house became known as an English chop house, and was in the main patronized by Yorkshiremen who were engaged temporarily in selling manufacturers' consignments and remitting the proceeds in cotton or gold. Yorkshiremen have always been distinguished for their clannish tendency, and have ever been noted for their devotion to Old England, so they congregated at Clark & Brown's to enjoy the nearest approach to their native diet which the place of their exile afforded. They made it a species of Exchange—met to talk over business, and, on the arrival of a packet, a rendezvous to communicate news from home. It was at this hour that the nucleus of the St. George Cricket Club was formed, and from which the players started to participate in a game on their ground located on Broadway, where the magnificent Gilsey House now stands. The upper dining-room rang with boisterous merriment when on extraordinary occasions they convened to bid adieu to one of their countrymen, who, having arrived poor and a stranger, had succeeded, by the tact for which the race is so celebrated, in amassing an ample competency, and was on the eve of sailing from the inhospitable Yankee shore to spend his American gold at home. At these gatherings, the beef, the mutton, the pudding, the ale, the bread, the cheese, even the celery and salt, were pronounced inferior to the glorious fare so abundant at Huddersfield or Saddleworth. The "blarsted" country was awarded the accustomed sneers, and the lucky one who had secured his pile was warmly congratulated that his pilgrimage was ended. "May we all be fortunate enough to follow suit at an early day," was drank with all the honors. Buckley Bent, John Bradbury, John Taylor, William Bottomley, Samuel Lord, and a host besides who has migrated with but a beggarly amount of capital, have all returned to astonish cousins and gaping neighbors with their princely fortunes.

The Auction Hotel, so christened on account of its proximity to the stores of the well known houses of John Haggerty & Sons, Wilmerding & Co., L. M. Hoffman, etc., was on Water Street near Wall. From its inception it was strictly an American eating-house, and though dignified by the title of hotel it never rose above the proportions of a dining-hall. As such it became celebrated for its varied bill of fare, which included all the favorite dishes then in vogue, and its highly prized home made pies were temptingly displayed on a long counter, already sliced for the customer who had no time to ask questions; barely sufficient to help himself; bolt the delicious article; throw down his shilling, and rush out. George W. Brown was the proprietor, a worthy citizen, and it might be a slur on his memory to hint that in order to build up a prosperous trade he in any way forestalled the great American showman who gained a wide-spread reputation through his advertising dodges. Brown had been a merchant in the city but had failed (when suspension was not the light affair, so easily arranged in one day,) and rumor has it, resorted to this enterprise to build up his broken fortunes. So the story ran. Certain it is he was successful in accumulating a large amount of money, but the second chapter of this romance is narrated in glowing terms as follows: After a season of unprecedented success he invited all his old business creditors to a sumptuous repast spread in an upper room of the "Auction." They all came, of course, and each was provided with a seat at the loaded table. As one after another unfolded the damask napkin placed before him by the polite host, a sealed envelope was disclosed duly addressed, which when opened was found to contain a check for principal and interest of their respective claims. It matters little now whether the story be true or false; it obtained credence at the time, and men flocked to spend their dollars with the honest landlord.

Downing's was another of the same class but of a different type. This once famous cellar was located at No. 5 Broad Street, and occupied the basements of two small buildings. Its proprietor was a negro, and his place was frequented by those who believed in the marked superiority of colored cooks. Oysters, always in great favor with New York epicures, Downing made a specialty, and these served with great care in the most approved styles, formed the leading article of his traffic and established his reputation. This unattractive cellar, so far as adornment was concerned, was more of a lounging place than the others named from its close proximity to the Custom House, then running through from Pine Street to Cedar, finding ample accommodation within the limits of the medium sized stores, the Merchant's Exchange and the prominent banks. Leading politicians also made it headquarters, dropping in to have a chat while enjoying their half dozen Saddle Rocks or Blue Points. Samuel Swartwort, the generous-hearted but unfortunate Collector of the Port; William M. Price, the hospitable and learned District Attorney; John-John J. Coddington, afterwards Postmaster; Abraham R. Lawrence, President of the then embryo Harlem Railroad, running from Prince Street and the Bowery to Yorkville Hill, where its progress was stopped during the excavation of the then famous tunnel; (how famous it was considered the following, written at the time by a leading journalist, will testify: "This tunnel at Yorkville is said to be as spacious as any other excavation of solid rock made in modern times, not excepting the excavation of the Simplon by order of the Emperor Napoleon, and the approach to it at both ends is an object not less interesting than the tunnel itself. There is scarcely to be found more beautiful and picturesque scenery in any part of the world than the view Hell Gate and its surroundings present to the eye from the embankment north of the tunnel. This great work is still far from completion, though the energetic management of the Harlem Road are not sparing of their means, and their aim is to reach Harlem River at the earliest possible moment.") This Harlem Road met its first check at Yorkville Hill; that was indeed a hard one to overcome, but in time it bored its way through the rock and reached its original point of destination. Since then, however, it has met with far more depressing obstacles to its progress. In its early stage it became a favorite foot ball in Wall Street, where its worthless stock was tossed about as a plaything, valueless as a security in time of need. After George Law, Philo. Hurd, and heaven only knows who else, had run it deep in the mire of discredit, Commodore Vanderbilt by a series of manœuvres executed with fidelity by his man Friday, John M. Tobin, acquired possession of the wreck and has given it position among the leading roads of the country. It certainly did not look promising as an investment to those who in its early days walked up to Vauxhall Garden, opposite where the Cooper Institute now stands, to witness the departure of a train for the remote region of Harlem. This train consisted of two elongated boxes mounted on tiny wheels propelled by a locomotive about as powerful as a modern tea kettle at *full boil;* the backing and filling required to compass the up grade at the point now covered by Union Square was ridiculous in the extreme, for on a dead level the machine could easily have been distanced by the Commodore's trotters, Mountain Boy, Myron Perry or Daisy Burns—but enough of this digression; Bobby White, the rotund, cheerful President of the Manhattan Co., which supplied us with *tea water*, at a penny per pail, from the great reservoir on Thirteenth Street near the Bowery; Jacob Barker, quaker, banker, broker, speculator in general; James B. Glentworth, the pioneer of political pipe layers and Inspector of Tobacco; Fitz Greene Halleck, bookkeeper for John Jacob Astor, the author of "Marco Bozzaris," "Fanny," etc., and the friend of Drake, Leggatt & Bryant; Wilmerding & Jones, the witty auctioneers; Gentleman Jack Haggerty, George L. Pride, John H. Coster, Stephen Whitney, Ham Wilkes and a host of other good men-about-town found time amid their varied duties, schemes and pleasures to dive down the steep cellar steps to take a peep at Downing and have a few moments cheerful chat.

With such surroundings Downing naturally became the medium of communication from one customer to another. The messages in the main were doubtless trivial and insignificant; but the fact invested him in the eyes of the public with no inconsiderable amount of importance, and by degrees it was whispered about that the oysterman had influence at the Custom House, Post Office and City Hall. These rumors had the effect of drawing many office-seekers to the cellar, who treated him with the marked respect usually bestowed on the power behind the throne. But it was lucky for Downing that in his day offices were few and patriots far less importunate than now; the rumor would have been a malicious practical joke if he had been compelled to face the insatiate horde which at present besieges every minute crevice through which public pap can possibly ooze. Downing after the lapse of years became what was then called rich, but had the good sense to keep pace with progress, and not to allow his quondam aristocratic associates to blind him with reference to his real position. Up to the termination of his career as caterer he was studiously civil and attentive to all classes of customers, and at a ripe old age he assigned his title "Prince of Saddle

Rock" with "the tenements and hereditaments thereunto belonging" to his son George T. Downing, who on assuming the reins of power attempted to mingle a sprinkling of politics with his unsurpassed bivalves, and thereby illustrated the truth of the old proverb "that a little learning is a dangerous thing." George did not graduate a Fred Douglas in his high flown aspirations; he was used some by the demagogues, but has always been compelled to mingle oyster stews and politics together to eke out a subsistence. He migrates between Washington and Newport in the prosecution of his two-fold occupation, and had he chosen, like the wise cobbler, "to stick to his last," his substantial success would have been greater and his social position just about as elevated.

Edward Windust was the proprietor of a saloon, which so far as associations were concerned, had no competition in the city. Its location was in a basement on Park Row, only a few steps South of the Park Theatre. It was a theatrical rendezvous; newspaper men, actors, artists, musicians, with that innumerable throng of needy admirers which always follows in the wake of shiftless genius, made it for years their headquarters. Over the Park Row entrance to this cave, for by some tortuous winding it had an egress on Ann Street, there was displayed a sign bearing the motto "*Nunquam non paratus*," and in consequence there were repeated applications by itinerant venders to interview either Mr. N. or Mr. P.; be that however as it may, Windust was a host widely known, and his rooms each evening between the acts and after the performance were filled with the wit and talent of the city. Ranged on one side of this underground resort was a tier of boxes or stalls, in each of which six could comfortably sit and partake of a well prepared supper. Many a jovial party was accommodated in these nooks, and if the old partitions could be gifted with speech what riches of joke and repartee might be given to the world, which are now forever buried in oblivion.

The walls of this sanctum were covered with reminiscences of the stage; portraits of the great delineators of character and passion who have passed away, quaint old play-bills of an antedeluvian age; clippings of criticisms carefully preserved as mementoes of misty traditions, contributed by some sock and buskin antiquary to perpetuate the memory of his own brief career; the sword with which Garrick was supposed to have committed his histrionic murders amid the plaudits of thousands; in fine, it was the actor's museum of New York. Cooper, Cooke, Edmund Kean, Junius Brutus Booth, The Wallacks, Tyrone Power, Thomas S. Hamblin, Jack Scott, Harry Placide, Peter Richings, John Fisher, Mitchell, Brown, Billy Williams, and a host of other theatrical lights, with Park Benjamin, George P. Morris, N. P. Willis, Parke Godwin, Dr. Porter, Massett, Dr. Bartlett, of the *Albion;* McDonald Clarke, the crazy poet; Price, the manager; Jim Otis, Fitz Green Halleck, George A. Dwight, and their *confrères* of the pen, met here on mutual ground of good fellowship, and over the foaming tankard nightly buried the hatchet, which always has and always will be flourished defiantly by the antagonistic forces of the stage and press. Pages of recollections might be related of each night's sayings and doings at the "Nunquam Non Paratus;" how the erratic Booth and the fiery Kean had ensconced themselves in one of the boxes and indulged in wild debauch during their joint engagement at the Park, to the inexpressible agony of the mild Simpson, who, like the matronly hen, clucked frantically at nightfall in search of the pets, that he might gather them in, but how they would not be gathered in until the landlord's score was liquidated, which the frightened manager was only too glad to do, as it was near the hour for the curtain to rise, and the great Othello and Iago would require the intermediate time to be cooled off sufficiently so as not to travestie the tragic master-piece into a ridiculous farce; how Jack Scott, with his broad chest expanded, his eye rolling with melodramatic frenzy, his ample shirt-collar unbuttoned to afford full play to his massive throat, raved at the scared critic who had dared to assert that Edwin Forrest ever had or ever could have an equal; how Tom Hamblin tossed his flowing locks when declaiming, in ecstatic tones, the glorious qualities of the gifted Josephine Clifton; how Hilson raised a roar by merely hoping "he did not intrude," as he awoke Charles Kemble Mason from his reverie on the majestic Fanny Kemble; how Robert Macaire Brown and Jacques Strop Williams relieved Manager Mitchell of the original manuscript of the "Savage and the Maiden;" how Manager Price buzzed the ears of the critics with laudations of the great Vestris, and how carefully the wily Stager avoided the slightest approach to the age of that famous octogenarian who could sing "I am si-i-hix-hix-ty-two," as if it were not so at all; how Harry Placide would gloat over the ever varying humor of Mrs. Vernon, and affirm the Fisher family to be all prodigies, including the youthful Clara, the "spoiled child" of the day— but these *hows* come so thick and fast that the reader will forget the eating-house of Gotham. Windust waxed rich, but as the money flowed into his treasury he became restless with his confined limits, and, like most mortals, he craved a wider sphere of action, and about 1836 he opened the Athenæum Hotel, on the corner of Broadway and Leonard Street. This experiment lasted only for a time; it gradually dwindled until Windust was too glad to return to the place where his reputation was established, but only to find its prestige gone.

CHAPTER NINTH.

The café of the time was a very humble affair, still its existence was an evidence of growth and expansion. It affirmed that the European Continental element was becoming sufficiently important to demand its introduction, and by an unfailing law the supply was at hand. French and Italian citizens were few in number, so the consumption of "café noir" was very limited, and the enterprising men who had embarked in the business, were compelled to add the sale of candies and cakes to meet the moderate expenses thus incurred.

Delmonico and Guerin, so far as memory serves, were the pioneers in this peculiar branch of industry. Both were industrious, frugal, persevering men, professed cooks and confectioners, thus fully competent to meet any exigency and to profit by their skill.

The descendants and successors of Delmonico now occupy four costly and conspicuous buildings in the city; furnished with all the appliances that modern art can invent to pander to the luxurious taste of the time, and one of them, the corner of Fifth Avenue and Fourteenth Street, is, beyond all question, the most palatial café or restaurant on this continent. The stream of fashion which flows through its spacious apartments from morning until night, or rather, from morning until morning, amply demonstrates the source of the immense revenue required to move its intricate and expensive machinery. To lunch, dine or sup at Delmonico's is the crowning ambition of those who aspire at notoriety, and no better studio for character does the city afford than that expensive resort at almost any hour of the day. The indulgence of the whim may be depleting to a moderate purse, but the panorama once seen and carefully inspected in all its lights and shades will amply remunerate for the outlay of money, and the time will not be misspent. On entering from Fourteenth Street one cannot fail to be impressed by the absence of bustle and confusion, no boisterous commands are heard, and the waiters glide about as noiselessly as ghosts. An air of luxury surrounds you as the attentive "garçon" stands motionless before you, and respectfully awaits your wishes. The order once given, you have ample time to survey the scene. At the adjoining table is seated a grey-haired, soft treading "gourmand," who gloats over his "carte" as if "life and death were in the scroll," and everything depended upon the selection he was about to make ; farther on is seen a fresh fledged millionaire, who furtively glances about him as if in dread lest some old acquaintance may see him, or that some new made friend should not, as he points to his order for the highest priced item on the list, having no remote idea what compound will be placed before him, only knowing that the figure in the margin is large, and he awaits, with all the "sang froid" he can summon, the result of his venture, but resolved to attack it no matter in what shape it may appear; opposite to this ambitious Courtland Street graduate lounges a puffy dowager, crowded into the nearest approach to shape by her dressmaker. The much dressed dame is perspiring at every pore, with the dread lest some stay prove ineffective to longer resistance; beside her sits what, by universal consent, is called the "Belle of the Period," and to describe one would be to describe the class, but the mere idea is ridiculous to use an inelegant but expressive Yankee phrase, "the thing can't be did," for man has failed in every attempt to compass the portraiture of the nondescript. A woman of raw talent might partially succeed, but the inference is that even Fanny Fern would be convinced that her experience and facile pen were both inadequate to the task, and would be driven to woman's "dernier resort," a postscript, *i. e.*, for further particulars the reader is referred to a personal inspection of this unnatural curiosity. Nast can caricature men with tremendous effect, but all the shafts he has hurled at the modern city belle fall pointless; her *make-up* defies ridicule, it "out Herods Herod." In close proximity to the city belle are seated two fresh looking demoiselles, who evidently like yourself are strangers to the scene, and are so absorbed in scrutinizing what has so much puzzled your brain that they have apparently forgotten themselves, for their lunch remains untouched before them, while their eyes are riveted upon her as if counting each stitch in the innumerable array of frills, flounces and tucks prescribed by fashion. So there is no danger of detection by indulging in a somewhat minute comparison. These country girls, evidently of no mean pretensions, have chignons of considerable proportions, but they are mites when compared with the *pillion* of their city sister; their plentiful display of French jewelry pales before her varied assortment of flashing gems; air and exercise have tinted their cheeks with a delicate glow of health—high art has enameled her face with the choicest mineral shade; their eyes are sparkling with a natural lustre—restless dissipation has given her a cold, stolid stare, satiety and ennui in every outline and every movement; yet, strange to relate, when these country lassies had completed the critical analysis of this highly finished model of fashion, and their eyes fell upon their own neat but scanty embellishments, a half mortified expression of envious discontent spread over their innocent faces; they hurriedly applied themselves in silence to their lunch, and modestly withdrew as if dazzled by this unaccustomed glare. Woman is verily a puzzle.

At another table is a party of prinked-up young men, a collection of gaudy neckties, flash jewelry, and rapid pretense. These pride themselves on being *fast*, while in fact they are the dullest and slowest of mortals, and were it not for the amusement afforded by their ridiculous costumes, antics and grimaces, they would be hooted at by every true man and woman. This adjective *fast* has been taken up by Young America, female as well as male, and is used by them in lieu of the old-fashioned phrase "man of the world," which had and still has a deep, decided significance, and no upstart parvenu can for a single moment disguise himself so as to escape detection. The title, "man of the world," implies intellect, cultivation, grace of person, ease of manner, gentleness of tone, perfect self-control; in fine, a character so decided and so evenly balanced as never to be ruffled by petty crosses and annoyances. The dress of the man of the world is invariably suited to each occasion; he follows the style, but never leads it; it is perfect in its completeness, nothing striking in detail, everything "*comme il faut.*" His address, especially in the presence of ladies, although entirely free from awkward restraint, is characterized by modest repose; in conversation he eschews the personal pronoun, and perfectly understands when to lead, when to be led. How and in what respect, those noisy, *fast society men*, who are seated at that table, are entitled to the distinction they claim, they themselves must determine; that they are recklessly fast in squandering time, opportunity and means, no one will deny,—they certainly are very far from being Chesterfields or D'Orsays. The gambler's well-filled purse and politic lavish expenditure, insure his welcome here as elsewhere in the halls of fashion. His smiling face is known to all and his careless nods of recognition are returned from right and left as he leisurely saunters to his accustomed seat. His diamond is matchless for purity and size, his horses unequalled on the turf or drive, and so forsooth he is recognized by society. The lawyer seeks him for his client, the physician is prompt in attendance at his call, the tradesman bustles at his nod, and the politician courts his powerful influence,—in his case all antecedents are ignored.

But it is needless to catalogue the scenes at Delmonico's in 1870, its frescoed ceilings, mirrored halls, and sumptuous appointments are too familiar to warrant description. The thousands who go there to see, and the tens of thousands who are straining every nerve to be seen there, may possibly be more interested by a brief outline of Delmonico's, as established during the last days of Knickerbocker regime. In a small store on William Street, between Fulton and Ann, directly opposite the North Dutch Church the now metropolitan name first became known to New Yorkers. The little place contained some half-dozen pine tables with requisite wooden chairs to match, and on a board counter covered with white napkins was ranged the limited assortment of pastry. Two-tine forks and buck-handled knives were not considered vulgar then, neither were common earthenware cups and plates inadmissible. As a matter of course the first custom was derived from the foreign element, attracted by the "fillets," "maccaroni," "café," "chocolat" and "petit verre." These were duly served by the "Chef" in person, who, with white paper cap and apron, was only too glad to officiate as his own "garçon." By slow stages the courteous manner of the host, coupled with his delicious dishes and moderate charges, attracted the attention, tickled the palate, and suited the pockets of some of the Knickerbocker youths who were on the lookout for something new, who at once acknowledged the superiority of the French and Italian cuisine as expounded and set forth by Delmonico. It must not, however, for a moment be thought, that the new converts from the plain roasted and boiled doctrine to the new rich gravy faith, plunged at once into the vortex of the elaborate and expensive spread, now every-day affairs at Fifth Avenue. By no means was such the case; their visits were at wide intervals and mostly confined to Saturday afternoons, when the good folks were almost certain to be at home laying out their Sunday clothes. Two or three would agree to meet at the Café for the purpose of indulging in a light French entertainment. On these occasions unusual secresy was indispensable, for if detected, we were certain to incur the marked displeasure of our grandmother, and to be soundly berated in the first place for our foolish extravagance, and secondly, pitied for our lack of taste by giving preference to "such vile greasy compounds," which we were assured would destroy our stomachs; while if we dared to mention the cool, refreshing *"vin ordinaire,"* that delightful beverage was denounced as a miserable substitute for vinegar. Still, in spite of the well-meant warnings we repeated our visits whenever we could do so with safety, and were warranted by our limited supply of "pocket money;" and yet farther, with what our old fogy ancestors would have pronounced unprincipled, we inducted others into the secret that good things to eat could be had at the little cook-shop on William Street. Gradually the little shop had not the requisite space to accommodate its increasing patronage, and Delmonico, instead of following the stream that pointed up-town, wisely removed his business still further down in the centre of the wholesale traffic before the disastrous conflagration of '35. When after a time that direful calamity was surmounted, he built the restaurant still standing on the corner of William and Beaver Streets, in which the brothers with their sons and nephews accumulated fortunes, and from which sprang the branches now so flourishing on the thoroughfares of New York.

Francis Guerin, a native of France and a cotemporary of the original Delmonico, opened his café on Broadway, between Pine and Cedar Streets, directly opposite the City Hotel, then the most busy portion of the leading thoroughfare. Keenly alive to the accumulation of dollars he ornamented his show windows to attract the attention of promenaders and stragglers who continually passed to and fro before his shop. His display consisted of imported and domestic confectionery, inviting specimens of pastry and cake, bottles of choice French cordials, fancy boxes filled with Parisian bon-bons interspersed with the fruits then in market. Inside, the shelves were lined with preserves in sugar and brandy while on a long counter, which reached from end to end, were spread the tarts and confections for which the place was noted until a very short time ago. From its location and limited dimensions this place was never, strictly speaking, a café or restaurant; sandwiches, sardines, and the sweets mentioned constituted the daily bill of fare, although at the rear of the store a small apartment was furnished with table and chairs, where coffee, chocolate, and, in Summer, ice cream, were served; but it was at best a dingy place, and as it had no entrance except through the store, it was but little frequented, and never by ladies. After a limited period the pie and cake counter was curtailed and the confectionary department became merely ornamental, except during the holiday season, to make space for the bar, which was lengthened and widened at the expense of the other branches,—for the retailing of liquors grew into the prominent feature of the business. Essentially it degenerated into a cosmopolitan drinking saloon, where Americans rushed for their hurried nip of brandy-and-water, Frenchmen sauntered about sipping absinthe and orgeat, Italians smacked their lips over a thimblefull of maraschino,—for all nationalities claimed to find at Père Guerin's their favorite beverage in perfection. From this trade a fortune was soon realized, but the proprietor had no ambition for display and very little love for even cleanliness; he spent nothing in repairs or renovation, and the old place became dingy through neglect, though it continued in the hands of a successor to drive a brisk trade until two or three years ago, when its site was required for more remunerative improvements, when the old crib was demolished "leaving no trace behind."

Delmonico and Guerin, though starting simultaneously in the same business, and though both were successful in amassing wealth, were, as proved by results, very different men in temperament and design. The former a generous, enterprising Italian, while he adhered strictly to his original plan, enlarged and improved when warranted by the demand and the growth of the city. A social host, his ambition was to please the public, and to outstrip competition by a lavish yet judicious expenditure. He rose from the obscurity of a petty shop and lived to have his name known everywhere, at home and abroad. The latter, a Frenchman of penurious tendencies, with no personal ambition, stuck to his shop, accumulated an immense estate, but so far as the public knows has left no record to tell when or how he had lived and died. The old sign "Francis Guerin, Confectioner," has been swept away.

CHAPTER TENTH.

The promenade was Broadway, the extremes being Bleecker street and the Battery. Though the bustle was great in proportion to the population, it was a quiet lane in comparison with our surging thoroughfare bounded by the same limits. The sites now covered with costly piles of marble or granite, ornamented in the highest style of art, were occupied by modest three-story brick buildings, whose only adornment consisted of bright green blinds, with shining brass knockers and door-plates. Many of them below Park Place had been converted into retail stores or shops for fashionable tradesmen, for Broadway was becoming prominent for its styles and prices, and the beau of the day was not properly attired who did not patronize these self-appointed dictators of fashion. Wheeler, Tryon & Derby, Brundage or Elmendorf must furnish his clothes, his boots must be manufactured by Kimball & Rogers, a St. John hat was indispensable, and his satin stock was far from being "*the thing*" unless obtained at the furnishing store of Clark & Saxton. As a natural sequence, the young men who aspired to be considered as "sans réproche" in their toilets became mere tailors' blocks, as they were dressed in such uniformity of style, as effectually to destroy all individuality. From the prescribed style no departure was permitted, the tall and thin, the short and stout were forced to don l'habit de mode. No matter how unbecoming or uncomfortable, there was no redress.

Black was the prevailing color; it was worn for promenade, parlor, church, ball, business—in fact, every man who pretended *to dress*, dressed in "the inky habiliments of woe." No gentleman considered himself, or was considered by others, duly presentable who was not attired in a high, black beaver—not one of our modern, light, shining silk affairs, but a heavy, long-napped, broad-brimmed, bell-crowned hat, which pressed like a vice on the head; a broad, black satin stock, so wide and unyielding that the ground could only be seen three paces to the front, a species of military invention to enforce the order of heads up; a sharp-pointed, standing shirt-collar, in design not unlike the cutwater of a steamboat—no girl could kiss the wretched wearer without endangering her eyesight—and so large as to half conceal the beardless face of the man; a black frock coat, a marvel of disproportion and discomfort, short-waisted, narrow-chested, long, narrow skirts, with sleeves so tight as seriously to obstruct circulation, and to render bursting imminent should the dashing young man have occasion to use his arms; black pantaloons, tight to the skin, and so securely fastened by straps beneath the boot as to entirely destroy the free action of the knee for the purpose of easy locomotion; a prolonged sitting posture, when encased in these inexpressibles, was equal to a slight attack of paralysis. This discomfort was materially enhanced by a pair of Kimball's boots, high-heeled, narrow and pointed, and were only got into after a deal of labor, assisted by boot-hooks and soap. Black gloves and a black cane about completed the costume of the tortured exquisite, who imagined himself an Adonis.

These primitive dandies were deprived of one great source of pleasure enjoyed by the young men of to day, *i. e.*, they could not laugh at each other's folly, or criticise each other's lack of taste —they were all " black crows "—all were in straight jackets, but all were harmless members of society.

The belle was a little less restricted in the selection of color, but not a whit in the prescribed style, and was permitted small scope for the display of youthful charms, especially on the promenade. The conventional bonnet was so hideous contrivance in size and shape that " the old woman who rode on the broom " adopted it at sight, and a look at one of *"the frightful things"* would cause a shudder to pass through the delicate frame of a modern demoiselle. In shape this monstrosity was not unlike a coal scuttle, and was usually trimmed with a full-blown peony or a prodigious bunch of roses displayed on its ample crown. This grand affair was a most effective bar to anything approaching to a side glance "en passant;" far more effective than a gig top, for the latter could be lowered at will, while the former, when once adjusted, was a stationary fixture.

The antiquated, solemn appearance imparted by this *hat* was materially aided by the plain cloak or shawl which hung rag like and unadorned from the shoulders of the fair wearer, and which completely concealed any charm of figure or grace of outline which the timid maiden might possess, while a plain, untrimmed skirt, reaching only to the ankle, left unhid hose of spotless white, but, at the same time, did not hide from view a heelless, flat "slipper," kept in place by black strings wound around the ankle, durable, no doubt, but certainly not fascinating to the eye. A parasol, edged with deep, heavy silk fringe, and ponderous, carved ivory handle was always " en régle," and a bag of gay colored silk or velvet, embroidered with beads, and having the capacity of a modern travelling satchel, was indispensable for full dress. The main "pièce de resistance," however, was the handkerchief. This all-important article was, as a rule, bordered with lace, the quality of which was supposed to definitely fix the financial status of the family; and that its full glory might be displayed, it was carried by its exact centre between the fore finger and thumb, so that no speck of its size or jot of its value should be lost to the world.

The appearance of a bride on Broadway was a special relief from the monotony which characterized the otherwise humdrum promenade. As a matter of course the head gear of the bride was "a la mode," so far as shape and dimensions were concerned, but the thing was made of gorgeous white satin, and the high steeple crown was festooned with orange blossoms, and from the peak of the monstrosity was suspended a white veil of flashy blonde lace which nearly touched the ground, and so capacious in width as to envelope the fair one in its folds. The culmination was in the pearl brocade dress, which apparently contained sufficient material for the construction of half a dozen modern robes; the sleeves were poetically styled "leg of mutton," which, when filled out by the interior appliances, which mean little brothers affirmed, were composed of "live geese feathers," imparted a fearful breadth of shoulder The waist, or "bodice," as it was then styled, looked as stiff and uncomfortable as steel and whalebone could make it, while the skirt was gathered on the waist to act as balance or equivalent for the bonnet and sleeves. A massive gold chain was coiled around the neck, having a pendant of sufficient length to secure a gold chronometer, which was slipped into the belt, the latter being secured in front by a buckle of magnificent proportions. This conventional bride, all in white, with this conventional groom all in black, were interesting sights on Broadway when New York was forty years younger than to-day.

Before taking leave of these belles and beaux it is appropriate to briefly notice a place of resort during summer afternoons, which was considered not only fashionable, but eminently proper for them to patronize, into which they could boldly enter, sit down, and partake "sans peur et sans réproche." The New York Garden, Contoit, proprietor, was on the west side of Broadway, between Leonard and Franklin streets. This garden was a long, narrow plot, so densely shaded that no ray of sunlight could penetrate it, and on that account should have been patented as a refrigerator, for it often was *too* delightfully cool for health, and so dark that, on the approach of evening shades, the gloom was rendered more palpable by innumerable small glass globes, filled with sperm oil, in each of which floated a minute taper; these were suspended on the lower branches of the trees, and when duly lighted emitted an effulgence about equal to the same number of June bugs. On either side of the walk was ranged a tier of neatly white and green washed boxes; a board table ran through the centre of each of these tiny cubby holes, with seats to accommodate about four persons, but if very intimate friends, six could in an emergency squeeze in and manage after a fashion. Colored waiters, with white jackets and aprons, bustled hither and thither, as only excited darkies can bustle, supplying the eager crowd with vanilla or lemon ice cream, pound cake, or lemonade, then comprising the dainties to which the belles were restricted. This being a fixed unalterable fact, a young man of the period with three shillings in his pocket could invite a fair friend to enter the enclosure, to be seated in a box, and give her order without fear of discomfiture, for he knew his capital was fully equal to the emergency.

One saucer of Contoit's cream was ample to satisfy the cravings of an ordinary appetite, as the quantity was materially greater than could possibly have been afforded with more costly surroundings; an uncovered board for a table, overspreading branches in place of frescoed ceilings, a plank instead of a walnut lounge, a chipped earthenware saucer and a black pewter spoon did not involve enormous outlay of capital, so the proprietor could afford, when milk and sugar were much cheaper than now, to serve a heaping allowance for a shilling of either vanilla or lemon, while sixpence was all he demanded for a good-sized slice of pound cake—not over rich to be sure—and no charge was made for attendance or for the tumbler of pure Manhattan spring water. Eighteen pence, under these circumstances, would nicely do the business; the man with thousands at command could do no more. Contoit's garden was on the temperance plan, no bar was to be seen, no liquor publicly sold; but there was "a wheel within a wheel," even there; and a quarter slyly dropped into a sable palm would ensure a moderate supply of cognac to be poured over the lemon ice, which gentlemen almost always preferred to the more luscious vanilla, to the great surprise of their fair companions, who frequented this place by the consent of their watchful parents and guardians; so the initiated and the smiling Sambo, our accomplice in the dark transaction, were compelled to be very shady. The manœuvres to elude detection were sometimes ludicrous in the extreme. Time has, however, removed the ban of secresy; garden, proprietor, parents, guardians have all passed away, and the girls, grown older, have become too well accustomed to modern usages to indulge in any upbraidings at this late day.

It has been mentioned that private residents were being fast driven from Broadway to make room for the retail trade. Cedar and Liberty streets, east of the thoroughfare, with Maiden

Lane, John and Fulton streets, were wholly given up to business purposes, and the houses on Cortlandt and Dey streets, were mostly occupied as boarding houses of a second class. Park Place, Barclay, Murray, Warren, Chambers and Beekman streets were tenanted by some of the oldest and best families. On the door-plates were seen such names as Bayard, Cruger, Allen, Brown, Lee, Clinton, Lawrence, Paulding, Ten Eyck, De Peyster, Van Cortlandt, Duane, Beekman, Graham, etc., whose descendants are among our most honored citizens. They were merchants who laid the foundations upon which we are now rearing our magnificent structure, and belonged to the class of men eulogized by Henry Earl, of Northampton, when he so eloquently said: "The merchant is a state and degree of persons, not only to be respected, but to be prayed for. They are the convoys of our supplies, the vents of our abundance, Neptune's almoners and fortune's adventurers." Some of this class had the enterprise to remove still further from the business portion of the city, and built themselves homes on Franklin, Leonard and White streets to make doubly sure that their seclusion would not be invaded by bustle and confusion. One old gentleman who loved his quiet was a long time undecided whether to select a plot on Broadway, or on Walker's Lane near Chapel street—the prices of both were the same—but after due deliberation he fixed upon the latter, for the avowed reason that the Post Road would always be dusty and noisy. Both spots are dusty now, but unfortunately for his heirs at law the Post Road lots are worth dollars while his deliberate choice would not realize cents in comparison.

White street was the natural passage to St. John's Park, and west of Broadway was soon lined with first-class brick dwellings. On the north side, close to Broadway, were the homes of the Depau family of daughters, distinguished for their beauty and wealth, as well as for their aristocratic descent, derived through their mother, Silvie, who was the daughter of the distinguished Comte De Grasse. These ladies, who had intermarried with the Livingstons, Costers, Fowlers, were justly considered as leaders in society, and their selection of White street stamped it for the time, and others rapidly followed in their wake. St. John's Park was a quiet but fashionable quarter for many years. The umbrageous enclosure was kept in perfect order, and, as it was private property, no one having access to it save those who occupied the surrounding houses and their invited friends, ladies and children could lounge or play in the ground free from all intrusion. The many cheerful games and romps enjoyed in the old Park are cherished recollections with hundreds of men and women, who felt unfeigned sadness to see the trees levelled and the old playground blotted out to make way for high walls and the shrill whistle of the locomotive. Only two or three of the door-plates now remain on the houses that faced the Park; the names of Lord, Kemble, Lydig, Coit, Monson, Berrian, Russell, Hosack, Binsie, Delafield, etc., are no longer to be seen there, and the descendants of the former parishioners of the old church have flown to more aristocratic and genial quarters; nothing but the church with its tall spire is left as a landmark of a past generation. Yes, one other, but of more modern date, remains—the church still standing on the corner of Laight and Varick streets, originally under the pastorate of the venerable Samuel H. Cox. This eloquent Presbyterian minister, who has been one of the bright lights of the New York pulpit for half a century, still lives, but though mellowed by age, is yet equal to the task of enchaining an audience by his thrilling flow of language when roused by the grandeur of his theme. In early life he was impulsive, by some considered erratic; his fast-rushing thoughts were not unfitly compared to chain lightning. He was among the earliest to embark in the Abolition movement, and as he did nothing by halves he brought on himself and on the church in which he preached a visitation from the riotous crew, who were opposed to this new political, religious crusade. He was hooted on the street and in the pulpit, and for a time suffered an eclipse, but he lived through the troublesome period, and has since had host of admirers, not to call them worshippers, of his transcendent talent.

But back again to our promenade, to take a glance at some of the characters of the time and become excited by the din of the stages that rattle over the cobble stones. There were individuals daily seen on Broadway who would be unnoticed in the present crowd, but at a time when each man knew his neighbor, when a strange face was remarked, an odd costume the subject of comment and much surmise, *Characters!* were objects of real interest. Prominent among them was McDonald Clarke, familiarly known as the "mad poet." He was of medium stature, far from unattractive in person, harmless and inoffensive in manner. His raiment was what would be termed "shabby genteel," but there was something magnetic about the man which especially excited interest in his behalf. He affected a careless, swaggering gait in keeping with his general make-up, and his unbuttoned "Byronic" shirt-collar looked peculiarly odd when contrasted with prim majority of his fellows. He lounged about the street, assuming an abstracted air, with his gaze fixed upon the pavement as if weighed down by some poignant sorrow. When audibly addressed by an acquaintance he returned the salute as if suddenly aroused from a deep sleep, and, after a faint smile of recognition, would relapse into his accustomed brown study. How does he live? was the oft-repeated question propounded by sympathetic woman. Would the unfortunate gentleman accept of some gratuity? was not unfrequently added, as the melancholy genius was on his accustomed tramp, intently seeking for something he was never to find on earth. McDonald Clarke never suffered for food while there was anything in Windust's storeroom, neither did he lack a few shillings to jingle in his pocket, for he unostentatiously mingled with the generous set, whose motto, "Let us live by the way," included the mad poet within its range. From time to time fugitive pieces over his signature appeared in print; they were all written in the love-sick, melancholy strain, and they confirmed the popular belief that unrequited love had clouded his brain. After his death some kind-hearted friend collected and published his verses, and humanely devoted the proceeds by erecting a monument to his memory in a secluded nook at Greenwood, where, after "life's fitful fever, he sleeps well."

Another character, but of a different type, was by common consent christened the Ginger-Bread Man. This singular specimen was a harmless lunatic, and mainly noticeable from the peculiar form his madness assumed. His name and history were unknown, and if he had relatives or acquaintances, even in the city, they never owned him before men; for no one has been seen to recognize or accost him on the street. This oddity derived the name by which he was known from his only visible article of diet, viz.: *Ginger Bread*. He was a man of powerful frame, with a ruddy countenance, denoting the highest health, and would be pronounced agreeable to look at. His dress was invariably a rusty black suit, discolored by continuous profuse perspiration, for he never was seen to walk Summer or Winter, but was always on a round jog-trot, as if intent on some mission of vital import. The pockets of his dress or "swallow-tail" coat were used as receptacles for his food, and seemed to contain an inexhaustable supply of the ginger cake upon which he made continuous drafts, which were passed to his mouth with an eager motion, indicative of craving hunger. His course was up and down Broadway, never stopping, except when one of the tea-water pumps was reached, where he would regale himself with a bountiful draught of pure spring water, refill his capacious mouth with the chosen staff of life, and start afresh on his crazy tramp, after *that* something which always seemed to be a little ahead of the unfortunate but determined creature. All at once he was missed from his accustomed place. One enquired of another as to his probable whereabouts. No one knew, so the Ginger-Bread Man passed away as he had lived—an unsolved mystery.

A third common, yet uncommon sight, was a weird member of the human family, who, by reason of always being covered with lime from head to foot, was appropriately designated as the Lime-Kiln Man. This tall, gaunt, cadaverous figure was usually clad in the loose cotton garb of a laborer, bespattered with lime; his uncut, uncombed locks were matted by constant contact with the same material, which also besmeared his long attenuated face and imparted to his "tout ensemble" a haggard expression not easily obliterated. Though he was the personification of the most abject poverty, this singular mortal was not a professional beggar; he was never known to solicit alms on the street or elsewhere, and he even gave no heed to the gaze of those who with pitying eye looked upon him as a fit object for succor; but instead, he stalked demurely on, as if unconscious of all surroundings. From what nationality he sprang, upon what means or special charity he subsisted, was never divulged. All the speculations about his being some distinguished exile, etc., were only nursery tales that excited wonderment among the prattling Knickerbockers. After some years of mysterious sojourn in our midst, the singular apparition was found dead in a lime kiln on the banks of the Hudson, which rumor asserted had been his nightly resting-place. At his death, the papers furnished the usual number of conjectures as to his antecedents and habits of life, but they were fancy sketches having no foundation in fact.

Dandy Cox was still another of our Broadway sights. This Cox was a good-looking, showy mulatto, who had selected the occupation of renovating gentlemen's clothing as a means of support, and to all outward appearance had a thriving trade. He was a caricature on the ruling fashions of the time, and with the *aping* propensities of his race was most successful in taking off the notables who affected *style*. Cox drove a spirited horse, sometimes hitched to a light wagon, but more frequently to a two-wheeled Stanhope, then considered an elegant vehicle, but which now would be considered as a *horse killer*, and entitled to the instant attention of President Bergh. He was always alive to the fact that he was a primary object of attention, and, darkey like, was equal to any emergency. His seat was as high pitched as possible, his well-brushed beaver cocked at the precise angle, his green jockey coat carefully arranged, so as to display every brass button, his wash-leather gloves spotless, his whip held by the centre, after the most approved cockney style, his elbows well up to gain a surer purchase on the fractious steed—his little nigger playing the tiger with the marked ability of a monkey—in fine, no modern nostrum vender can vie with Dandy Cox, if viewed in the light of an advertising medium. All the newspapers of his day could not have added one jot to his fame.

CHAPTER ELEVENTH.

Gotham had stages or omnibuses, few in number, but that deficiency was amply compensated by their proportions and decorations. These imposing conveyances were severally named after celebrated men and women, and it was considered not an every-day affair to take a ride in the George Washington, Lady Washington, General Lafayette, Benjamin Franklin, De Witt Clinton, Thomas Jefferson, etc., for their names were emblazoned on the sides in "characters of living light." These ponderous ambulances were propelled by four prancing steeds, and the several "*whips*" who engineered them were well-known to every urchin who pretended the slightest claim to respectability, for these men were looked up to as important personages in our little world.

The route for the Broadway lines was from the Bowling Green to Bond street, but if it chanced to rain very hard, and there was a lady in question, the courteous "*Yorke*" would gallantly drive his four *creams* as far north as the Kipp Mansion, then on the site now occupied by the New York Hotel. These celebrated stages did not all belong to one man; there were three distinct proprietors, and there was no inconsiderable rivalry, which fact invested them with an unusual amount of interest, engendered by their strife for popularity and patronage. Wicked little boys would bet apples that Brower's General Washington would beat Jones' Thomas Jefferson, and find takers that Colvill's Benjamin Franklin would distance the pair, so that on a Saturday afternoon Broadway became a race course on a moderate scale, and the unfortunate losers were twitted on their lack of judgment in horseflesh, or their folly in putting faith in certain tricky or incompetent drivers.

Abraham Brower's stables were on Broadway, opposite Bond street, mere shells of sheds running through to Mercer street, for anything was then considered good enough for a horse, and his one or two carriages and wagons had become weather-proof from long exposure. Evan Jones housed his stages on White street, while Colvill held out on Grand, just east of Broadway, where he was so cramped for space that Benjamin Franklin and De Witt Clinton were compelled to rest out doors after their daily labor. Land was cheap, like the Irishman's potatoes, but capital was limited, and the livery business a risky undertaking, though it was a well-known fact that if a gentleman who did not own an establishment desired to drive out with a lady, he was compelled to scour the city and give a day or two's notice to secure one of the few vehicles that a fair one would be willing to ride in during daylight. The fare on these Broadway lines was one shilling, but it was not, as at present, passed up through a hole, to reach which a man is compelled to take unwarrantable risks, either endangering his own limbs or else inflicting serious injuries upon the understandings of fellow passengers. The shilling was handed on entering or leaving to a small boy perched outside at the end of the stage, who acted in the capacity of a modern car conductor. Whether this youth divided square, i. e., between the proprietor, driver and himself, is not known. History is silent on this point; but certain it is that no great wealth flowed into the coffers of the trio who battled for the privilege of riding people up and down Broadway at a shilling apiece.

There was yet another stage line, which started from the corner of Pine and Nassau streets, through Broadway to Canal, from thence wandered away up Hudson street, past gardens and meadows, until at last Greenwich Village was reached. These accomodations came to a dead *Whoa!* at Charles street, where was the stable of Asa Hall, who, between making hats in Greenwich street near Dey, and carrying people in his stages at twenty-five cents each, became "*full handed*," and sold out the Greenwich line to two young enterprising men, who afterwards became prominent as the firm of Kipp & Brown. Few men of his day were better known or more widely respected than the genial, warm-hearted Sol Kipp. His purse was always open in response to the call of charity; his name at the head of subscriptions; in fun or frolic Sol was on hand, well knowing that his bright face and white cravat would receive a hearty welcome in any gathering of his fellow citizens. Though lavish in expenditure, ample means seemed ever at his command to gratify a wish or relieve a friend in distress, and it was not until the projection of the Eighth Avenue Railroad, which covered the whole line of his remunerative route, that misfortune overtook him. For years, in connection with his patrons, he battled in the courts against the rich monopoly, but finally George Law and his millions told against him in the scales, and Kipp found himself poor and of course friendless. This generous man who was for so long a period the life and soul of the "Village" where, in prosperity, his will was law, can now occasionally be seen tottering with age along Hudson street. unnoticed by the passing crowd and, sad to say almost unknown in a neighborhood where only a few years since he was greeted with a smile of recognition by every youngster who played marbles or spun a top in the district.

On the north-east corner of Broadway and Grand Street stood the Broadway House, a much frequented barroom which derived its chief patronage from the fact that the place was the Whig headquarters of the city and county when that party held power, and its committee dispensed the Federal and State patronage. At that time such men as Cadwallader D. Colden, Philip Hone, Walter Brown, Gideon Lee, Cornelius W. Lawrence, Aaron Clark, Joseph N. Barnes, the father-in-law of Oakey Hall, Nat Blunt, Frederick A. Tallmadge, Moses H. Grinnell, William Paulding, Philip W. Engs and others "nobile fratrum," were leading politicians, and were sought for to accept office at the hands of their constituents. There always has been wire-pulling in politics, hot-brained partisans, noisy followers in the ranks of faction; money was always required to work the machinery, and on the near approach of election stump orators were in demand, as well as quantities of "the ardent" to excite hope and brighten the blaze of patriotism. All this was so even in Knickerbocker times; still up to the close of Knickerbocker rule the rough and rowdy had no part or lot in the political organization of the day, and the nominees for positions were selected with reference to their fitness and qualification for office. Honor, not salary or fees, was the aim of candidates, and, even strange as it may appear to-day, the prefix of Alderman to a man's name did not imply that he was an adept in schemes to enrich himself at the expense of every manly attribute. Better still, in Knickerbocker days a seat on the Bench was a proud position; it was coveted by the wisest and best men at the bar; it was an independent tenure, free from the entanglements incident to nominations at primary meetings, and it was unembarrassed by promises and associations which must too often shield the guilty and thus defeat the ends of justice.

"Here's to you, Harry Clay," was one of the rallying cries of the old line Whigs who met at the Broadway House for a grand *pow-wow*, when, in lieu of a calcium light, a tar barrel and a few pine knots served all the purposes of illumination, while the intricate tariff question was being ventilated by a pet orator, who had been introduced and endorsed as sound by Prosper M. Wetmore, ere he was lifted on some stray hogshead especially captured for the occasion by Bill

Harrington and Bill Poole who belonged to this aristocratic wing of patriots.

Clay and Frelinghuysen were the last great standard bearers of the old Whig party, and during that memorable canvass the Broadway House was thronged with their zealous adherents. On the day of election, as the returns were received from point after point, a Whig triumph seemed assured; the odds were *"Any thing you like,"* money flowed like water in and about headquarters—the excitement rose to fever heat, and the air resounded with wild cheers for Harry Clay, whose magnetic power made him not merely the idol of his own party, but of the country at large. When evening came, "assurance was doubly sure," and an impromptu procession was formed, and a yelling crowd swept up Broadway to bear the glad tidings to Frelinghuysen, who was temporarily stopping with a friend in Washington Place. The supposed Vice-President elect responded to the enthusiastic call, and the welkin rang with continuous cheers for the "Star of the West." During the night, sleep was banished from the city, for the Whigs were drunk with joy. With the morning light, however, came tidings that New York State had proved recreant to her promises, and success had hinged upon its vote. The jubilant Clay men soon subsided, and the hitherto quiet opposition noiselessly pocketed the long odds, flung out their banner from the flag staff of old Tammany, and chuckled merrily over their too sanguine adversaries. This defeat dimmed the glory of the Broadway House—its lights went out, that is to say, the leaders who had given it its prestige sought new and more promising pastures. Some affiliated with the Loco-focos, while the majority embraced the *"isms"* generated by the Abolition Clique, who had defeated Harry Clay in what was supposed to be his stronghold, and who have now risen to power as the dominant Republican party.

Vauxhall Garden, a favorite resort for the democratic masses, occupied most of the block of ground now bounded by Fourth avenue, Lafayette place, Fourth street and Astor place. This extensive plot was surrounded by a high board fence, with a main entrance on Fourth avenue, opposite Sixth street. It was tastefully laid out in garden walks, shaded by a fine growth of forest trees, and ornamented by beds of shrubs and flowers. Small neatly fitted up boxes to represent mystic bowers were ranged along the fences, for the special accommodation of female visitors who desired refreshments, while benches and chairs were scattered under the trees for the use of male patrons who chose to sip their brandy and smoke their *principe* in the open air. In the centre of the space a large wooden shed, scarcely worthy to be called a building, had been erected for the purposes of a show, and it was occasionally used by a strolling company of actors, who charged a small fee for admission. It was occasionally changed into an impromptu ball-room, but a rather questionable band of music, with some inexpensive fireworks to amuse the children, were the staple attractions of the place. Vauxhall was out of town, it was considered a healthy romping place, and as the price of admission was nominal and the charges for refreshments moderate, on fine afternoons and holidays it was crowded with women and children. As the city grew, it became a favorite spot for mass meetings of every description, and the stamping ground of the *buncombe* orators. It was the theatre of the Slievegammon excitement; it was there that Barnum began his earliest raids as the leader in humbug, and if dame Rumor speaks true, the celebrated mermaid, one of his crowning frauds, was manufactured in Vauxhall Garden under the critical eye of the Prince of Showmen. Lot by lot it was gradually shorn of its proportions; dwellings were erected on Lafayette place, and the owners of the ground found profit in small stores on the avenue, so that years before its final destruction it had dwindled into a mere billiard and drinking saloon, though it retained its original name to the end. Bradford Jones, a well-known popular host, was its last lessee; he endeavored to keep alive its ancient prestige by the aid of cheap concerts, negro minstrelsy and calico balls, but he was rewarded with only small returns, and soon after the Astor place riot, when the ill-advised partisans of Forrest and Macready so disgracefully distinguished themselves, and the Vauxhall billiard tables had served as a resting place for the mutilated victims of that murderous affray, its doors were finally closed, and Bradford Jones sought another field of labor.

Barnum's name recalls the fact that Knickerbocker New York could boast of two museums. The most imposing of these was the American, founded by John Scudder, and occupying the prominent site where the New York *Herald* building now stands. Its varied collections were displayed in four long rooms, each one hundred feet long, and from its observatory might be enjoyed some of the finest views of the beautiful bay and surrounding country. Peale's was situated on Broadway, opposite the park, and was a counterpart of the other in everything save dimensions. Both of these establishments were real museums, not designed as convenient rendezvous for intrigue, but clean, silent, systematic places for serious contemplation, and the study of the wonders and eccentricities of nature. Children on crossing the thresholds of these temples dedicated to science were awe-stricken by the sight presented, and clung tremblingly to their grandmothers for protection while gazing upon the trophies which had been culled from every nook of the civilized and barbarian world. These museums would have been pronounced duplicates by a casual observer. Each had on exhibition the wax presentment of Daddy Lambert, and this historic fat man was caged by well authenticated representatives of heroes, criminals and murderers, whose romantic or villainous deeds had long been immortalized in nursery rhyme; so this wax department, when each figure had been pointed out and duly described by grandmother, was a grand attraction to youthful pilgrims in search of knowledge. Next in order of interest came the horrible boa constrictors, who were cruelly fed before our eyes with innocent live chickens and rabbits. During the process of his snakeship's meal the ears of the terrified young ones were wide open to listen, as the bland keeper gave an accurate statement as to what these monstrous reptiles would do if they only had the chance, and we timidly calculated in primary rules of arithmetic what power of resistance the slim wire bars could offer should the boa resolve to change his steady diet and try a taste of baby by way of variety. So we slunk away from possible danger to feast our eyes upon the benign countenance of the Father of his Country, satisfied from early education that even his features on canvass were a sure protection against all assailants.

The portrait of Washington was surrounded by a bevy of notables: Napoleon, Franklin, Penn, Christopher Columbus, Jefferson, Madison, Sir Walter Raleigh, Queen Elizabeth, &c., backed up by way of nationality by the imaginary heads of Indian chiefs, who massacred and scalped our forefathers and *fore*mothers with their innocent babes, who had never done them any harm except to give them *fire water* and glass beads for their lands and rich furs. Next came a wonderful mummy, with the precise date of its sepulture marked on a piece of parchment, yellow with time or by reason of some chemical appliance. Indian war clubs, bows and arrows of curious workmanship, canoes of bark and hide, scalps of unfortunate pilgrims, dried bones of all sizes and shapes, ostrich eggs suspended from the ceiling, old pennies arranged in glass cases, a piece of the frigate Constitution, the signature of John Hancock, some specimens of Continental money, but any quantity of large and small stones duly labeled and designated in a body as *the Cab-*

inet of Minerals, over which our elders lingered long, and expatiated in grateful terms on the enterprise of the proprietor who gave them such a rare scientific treat at so little cost, i. e., twenty-five cents, children half price, and the latter were considered as such for a much longer period than in this advanced age,—a boy of eighteen in a long tailed coat and high hat would have been the butt of his companions.

Each of these museums prided itself upon the attractions offered by its Lecture Room, where at a stated hour in the afternoon and evening an enthusiastic professor of something would learnedly hold forth on a subject about which he knew but little, but well aware of the fact that his slim audience knew less if possible. If the writer is not greatly mistaken, the theory of mesmerism was first broached in this country at Peale's Museum; at all events, it is certain that it was in that lecture room he listened to a pale-faced, gold-spectacled individual, who ventilated himself in the same disconnected, nonsensical strain which is now characteristic of the modern professor of spirit-rapping necromancy—a strain which has at first befogged, and eventually destroyed so many generous, brilliant men and women, wrecked multitudes of once happy homes, and materially aided in populating the lunatic asylums of the country.

But neither Scudder nor Peale confined themselves to dark-lantern *isms;* they did not pay in those hard-working, practical days, when people gave a wide berth to everything which did not commend itself to sound common sense, so they were compelled to cater to the taste of that large class, who while they enjoyed occasional amusement, had been educated to the belief that the *theater* was "*the gate of hell;*" the term was used from the pulpit, and what the Dominie said, must be true. So the devil was "whipped round the stump," and grandfather and grandmother would take the children on Wednesday afternoon, for that was a stated school holiday, to the Museum Lecture Room, and the dear old people would laugh till they cried at the oddities and witticisms on that miniature stage, never for a moment dreaming that they had entered the portals of Inferno, and were surrounded by the fumes of sulphur and brimstone.

A popular celebrity of the time who was frequently engaged to appear at the Lecture Room was a comical genius named Hill, who was the acknowledged personator of the *darned, downcaster* stage Yankee, with short striped trowsers, long straps, lank hair, immense shirt collar, white hat, shuffling gait, jack knife, whittling stick and drawl. Hill's imitation was pronounced perfect, and by common consent he was long known as Yankee Hill. His performance was a monologue and was made up of long spun yarns: How Jonathan courted Charity Jones while peeling apples or shelling chicken feed by the kitchen fire; Deacon Swift's horse swap; Aunt Tabithy's tea scrape; Burlesque Fourth of July orations, interspersed with popular melodies sung with a peculiar nasal twang which elicited roars of laughter.

Daddy Rice, the originator of the now popular negro minstrelsy was another great card at the Lecture Room; his celebrated "Jump Jim Crow" was carolled by all the jolly boys and pert servant girls in Gotham and for many years these and similar entertainments sufficed to satisfy the patrons of the museums. By degrees, however, the strict barriers of demarcation were one by one withdrawn, and when Barnum became proprietor of the American, and Peale was absorbed, he enlarged the stage, expanded the dimensions of the Lecture Room and introduced one after another the dreadful appliances of the "Devil's School of Ethics" without disturbing the consciences of sensitive audiences, who could still go to the museum and laugh or cry over the veriest sensation trash, but would not dare to be seen in a temple devoted to the highest flights of the legitimate drama. Barnum discovered that pious dollars would purchase full as much in the open market as could be bought with an equal number which had passed through the grip of the ungodly. He crowded his Lecture Room by bringing out *high moral dramas* which he puffed as illustrated sermons in disguise, sugar-coated pills; and the numbers converted by them, at an outlay of fifty cents each, can be approximated by ascertaining the cost of Ivanistan and the value of the many prominent pieces of property in New York and elsewhere registered in the name of the distinguished temperance lecturer.

CHAPTER TWELFTH.

When the population of New York City was about two hundred thousand, *Society*, to use the word in its modern application, was not subdivided as at present. Active employment was a necessity for all men; sloth was a bar to respectability. There were some "retired men," as they are now styled; but as a rule extreme age or chronic infirmity was the cause which forced them to abandon an active life. The occupation, calling or trade of each man was known to his neighbor; for the mysterious ways by which fortunes are now gained without visible continuous labor, had not been discovered. Industry, punctuality, frugality, with a strict conformity to popular sentiment formed the basis of credit, which was all important to success, for this credit was the main capital of a large majority of merchants and tradesmen.

The city could boast of some few capitalists, but with the exception of two or three, where wealth was computed by hundreds of thousands, the principal of the balance would not equal the amount which thousands now expend annually in the maintenance of their princely homes. The church, the bar, medicine, the arts and sciences had each many eminent representatives in the community; men who were looked up to with that deferential respect which always has and ever will be awarded to those lives and talents are devoted to the study of social progress. Yet even these did not assume to constitute themselves into a Seclusion Coterie. The merchant came next, but the dividing line between *store* and *shop* was not so distinctly drawn as now; the status of employer and employee was less closely defined, the latter not unfrequently being an inmate, and ever a welcome guest at the home of his employer. Then came that large class known as mechanics, who with their journeymen, apprentices and laborers, has always formed so formidable a proportion of every city, and where success is mainly dependent on the demand for the thousand wants and luxuries which spring into being as labor accumulates capital. The simple necessaries of life require but little skill or toil for their production, and as *home* manufactures satisfied the Knickerbocker taste, fancy artificers met with only limited employment. Loungers or non-producers were marked persons at a time when "Early to bed and early to rise" was a ruling motto, and "to work while daylight lasts," was the governing habit from the learned professional man to the humblest artizan. Thrift, rigid conformity with social law, undeviating probity constituted the prime essentials to respectability.

Comfortable independence assumed cordial welcome by one class to the other, and really no aristocracy existed or was claimed, save where the distinction was cheerfully awarded to the cultivated and refined, but without the slightest reference to a pecuniary standard. There were circles naturally formed by congeniality of tastes and similarity of daily occupation which could not be entered by a mere golden key, the applicant for admission must possess the requisite affinities and bear about him the unmistakable evidences which, the world over proclaim the gentleman by sentiment and education. This idea of aristocracy pervaded Gotham and was derived from the staunch Knickerbocker stock; it underlied and formed the foundation of New York Society. The good old fathers and their *madames* were great sticklers for form and ceremony; their *ruffles* and *cuffs* were starched, and unwittingly imparted to the wearers an air of dignified composure that would check the merest approach to familiarity from their juniors, and kept even equals at a respectful distance. " Pater and Materfamilias" exacted the most implicit obedience from their offspring "even unto the third generation," while dependents and servants of every grade recognized Master and Mistress as if by intuition. This dignity was maintained even though they might be compelled to exercise the most rigid economy in the details appertaining to *home*. This home was an heirloom, not valued in the light of an estate to be converted into money, but priceless as having been the ancestral abode ; no matter how humble in dimensions or appointments. The idea of change in the massive, bulky furniture was never dreamed of, continuous use only made each familiar piece more highly prized: a fixed abode and a consistent, unvarying mode of living entered strongly into the Knickerbocker notion of family pride or aristocracy, they abhorred everything vaccilating, they looked with distrust on such as were here to-day and stayed somewhere else to-morrow, deeming they possessed no terrestrial anchorage upon which to base any claim to respectability. The social circle was made up from friendships rather than by mere acquaintances, and while there was no lack of hospitality there was a seclusive sanctity attached to the idea of home which bound it effectually against any who were not duly accredited as worthy.

Parental rule was supreme in the home and the power was not relinquished or even delegated while life lasted. It was founded on the patriarchal system; agreeable or distasteful it was law, and no juvenile quibble could avail in circumventing it. The head of the family reigned supreme in matters both great and small; in the kitchen and in the parlor; in income and expenditure; in fact, one brain and one purse regulated the domestic pendulum. Father or mother, or both, were in the parlor. The miss who had suggested the propriety of their spending the evening in dining-room or basement would, on the instant, have been awarded ample time for serious reflection in the seclusion of her chamber, and the *master in roundabout* had to make special arrangements of the most confidential character with *Betty*, as to which basement window should be left unbarred when the youth was seized with a freak of dissipation and had resolved to defy the ten o'clock mandate and stay out till eleven, for when the old clock on the stairs struck ten, guest or guests quietly departed, or they would have received a *demonstrative* hint by the closing of inside shutters and a general preparation to retire.

Parties, even among the most affluent, were not of frequent occurrence; stated reception days or evenings were not needed, for visiting had not been reduced to an empty ceremony. During usual hours and at proper seasons the ladies of New York were to be found at home ready to receive their friends, and if they were not attired in elaborate Parisian toilets, their unpowdered, blooming faces were wreathed with smiles of welcome.

On grand occasions, a wedding for instance, some pretentious preparations were indulged in; written invitations were issued, scientific outside aid was secured, so that Cornelia's bridal feast should compare favorably with that of her cousin Mary, which had been pronounced "*sans reproche*" by a jury of family *aunties*, who being relics of revolutionary sires were conceded to be posted, and from whose judgment in such, and in fact in all matters, there was no appeal. Even Jackson, the renowned colored caterer of the day, whose headquarters were in an obscure basement on Howard Street, and who assumed a thousand airs when waiting upon ordinary customers, most deferentially deferred to the dignified but firmly expressed opinions of these courtly dames; for if he had dared to differ from or oppose their wishes, these stately matrons could summon up a look and assume a manner and tone which would for the time have weakened a much more formidable individual than the pompous Jackson, who was, however, reported to take sweet revenge for these aristocratic snubs by lording it over those unfortunate customers who could boast of no *three-story aunties* who knew exactly what they wanted, and insisted upon not only having it, but in their own way, and not one word back.

Whittingham furnished the bridal robe, which custom ordained should be of white satin, with the slightest possible tinge of yellow to impart richness. The waist was styled a bodice, stiff and unyielding as its definition implies, terminating in sharp points before and behind, and laced to an almost stifling pressure. It was cut very low in the neck and shoulders and ornamented with a deep fall of rich blonde lace; the sleeves were tight and reaching only to the elbow, terminated by ample frills of lace extending to the waist; the skirt just touched the instep, but was so full behind as to rival the most imposing panier of a modern belle. Martell, *the coiffeur*, appeared on the scene early in the day to perform his part in the wonderful make up; by his skill he caused each particular hair to perform its whole duty, ere the three high-reaching bows on the top of the head were satisfactorily built up; and when the coronet of artificial orange blossoms, which sustained the blonde lace veil, was duly adjusted the sun was fast sinking in the West; so by the time Lane's white satin boots had been laced and the six buttoned gloves were worked on and secured, the bridesmaids, groom and groomsmen had arrived.

The bridesmaids were counterparts of their temporary mistress, save that their wreaths were of artificial roses, and no veil enshrouded the fair forms. The groom and his aids were magnificent in blue coats, brass buttons, high white satin stocks, ruffled shirt bosoms, figured satin vests, silk stockings and pumps, with their front hair tightly frizzed by Maniort in the highest style of tonsorial art.

Greenhouses were few and not over-abundantly stocked. One modern order would have swept them all for the season, and the extent of private conservatories was limited to a row of geraniums and monthly roses; in other words, limited by the capacity of the basement window sills, so that the floral display during Winter was far from being either extensive or extravagant. The enthusiastic groom was often compelled to make up the sad deficiency in the quality of his bridal bouquet by a lavish investment in the gilt and pearl holder which invariably accompanied it, for after diligent search among all the collections of plants in the family circle the precious thing culminated in a bountiful array of green leaves with a sickly rosebud or two as a grand central attraction. When such proved the insurmountable difficulty, the blushing bridesmaids were compelled to gaze abstractedly on their fans, which being of celestial Chinese manufacture, were profusely ornamented with the most elaborate counterfeits of rare exotics.

The lack of flowers and *nick-nacks* was amply compensated for by the substantial profusion of the supper table. The bride's cake, of formidable proportions, was the grand centrepiece. It was made at home, so solid and rich in its intricate composition that it improved by age, and it was cut into such generous slices and so liberally dispensed that a piece would serve for the dreams of a whole family. It was very different from the sickly looking substitute now immured in minute paper coffins, which so soon crumbles into tasteless dust. Solids and dainties were lavishly spread on the board; hams, chickens, turkeys, and often game, glass dishes of rich home-made preserves, high china fruit stands loaded with lady apples, oranges, Malaga grapes, raisins, nuts, mottoes made up under home supervision, the candy, Stuart's best, and the sentiments eminently proper; a towering form of Contoit's vanilla, brandy peaches of a flavor to make a temperance orator bound with joy, piles of cake of every known variety from the humble cruller to the most delicate wafer jumble. The dining room floor was not flooded with a reckless waste of champagne, though the sharp snap of the flying cork was heard distinctly amid the jovial din; Madeira, port and sherry were plentifully dispensed to enliven the marriage feast. Wax candles and astral lamps shed a mellow light from every nook where a silver candlestick could stand. All was life. Grandmother and our aunties were there, radiant in the full regalia of bygone days, stiff in ancient brocades, formidable in their towering caps, tortoise shell combs, powdered puffs and lace capes. Erect, composed, filled with self-esteem and self-assertion, they renewed their youth at these gatherings by a unanimous accord that earthly grandeur would pass away when they were summoned from the stage of life. It was a study to note the glance of disdainful pity with which they scanned the puny youngsters from the conceded post of honor, and at the same time exacting the most courteous attention from child and visitor. Better, perhaps, would it be for the present generation had that feudal system never been broken up; the restraints it imposed were morally healthful, for dignity instead of lawless frivolity reigned in the home circle when society paid deference to age.

There was a marked difference between an invitation "*to take tea*" and an invitation "*to spend the evening.*" Both signified that one should come early and not stay late; that is, come about seven and leave about ten. Neither involved the necessity of full dress, though the swallow tail coat was so common an affair that frock coats were the exception rather than the rule even for business, for the stereotype garment was worn for "Sunday go to meeting" and visits, until the seams presented a shiny appearance, when it was devoted to every day wear and was replaced by a new duplicate to serve its turn as "*very best.*" This invitation to take tea was an "*en famille*" entertainment, with some form, some ceremony, of course, but by contrast with the other it was informal and eminently comfortable. This evening meal, when the fire burned brightly in the cosy back parlor, was a delicious treat to the forlorn homeless bachelor, compelled to eke out an existence on boarding-house or even hotel fare. The tempting repast was artistically arranged on a highly-polished mahogany table, under the immediate superintendence of the young ladies who prided themselves on this domestic accomplishment. The family silver urns and service, burnished to the nicest point, looked grand when surrounded by the shining white and gilt cups and saucers; the cake basket fairly groaned beneath its pyramid of dainty varieties: the cut glass dishes filled with luscious sweetmeats flanked by shortcake, biscuit, toast, dried beef, tongue, cheese, all "*fixed*" in harmonious order. When all were duly seated around the inviting board, the fragrant steaming Bohea and Mocha had been poured out and distributed, each one having been asked, tea or coffee? sugar and cream? by the presiding lady of the domain, cheerful chat ruled, and a more delightful hour never fell to the lot of mortal man to enjoy. No bustle, no confusion, no hurry hither and thither of servants; simple, pleasant prattle—possibly the slightest imaginable sprinkle of the latest "*on dit*," but that was quickly restrained by a look from headquarters, lest any inconsiderate scandal should by the merest accident emanate from that family circle.

The female element usually predominated at the social tea parties, and no matter what special topics might casually be introduced, the great question raised in the Garden of Eden, what shall we wear? yet undisposed of, invariably came up for discussion. The dry goods stores were visited, patterns solicited, and, further still, the trade was then so limited that whole pieces of material and "nouveautés" of value were sent to the homes of customers and allowed to remain for days to be critically passed upon, so that the final selection should be a deliberate act, not to be repented of. As an illustration: A now prominent importer received two French Cashmere shawls, pronounced the most exquisite productions of the loom. The important fact soon became noised abroad, and to possess one of these treasures was the rage of the hour, for with the then ruling moderate tone, the wearer would be distinguished "not for a day," but through long succeeding years.

These much-coveted gems were by request sent to the residence of a lady, and after due deliberation were purchased by two friends who were leaders in society; one, the wife of a prominent merchant whose ancestors held high rank in the councils of the nation, and the other, the mother of a distinguished divine and Chancellor of the University. Both shawls are still in the possession of their respective descendants, and are exhibited with more pride than the endless variety of costly wraps which their unlimited wealth has enabled them to purchase. These cashmere shawls were worn with pride; why not? they were known to be the only ones in the city. Philosophers may sermonize on the folly and sinfulness of dress, but women pay but little heed to their lugubrious strains. Men may talk of "the lovely young Lavinia," so exquisitely unadorned, but when they are taken unawares by an elegantly dressed woman, their fine-spun theories vanish into thin air, and the coldest of them are forced to acknowledged that a well-ordered dress is a prodigious improvement to natural charms. Men do not pause to analyze their various emotions when in the presence of a woman they admire; but if like the botanist they should destroy the lovely vision to learn its structure, they would find that not a little of their impression was due to the well-arranged costume. Men of culture and refinement feel a sense of safety in the house of a well-dressed woman, which any amount of attention on the part of one carelessly attired would fail to engender.

The true woman knows by intuition that the secret of her power lies in appropriate costume, with decoration "costly as the purse can buy," and what woman is so conscientiously rich in personal magnetism that she can afford to lay aside the sceptre of her power? for nothing so stamps the personality, and imbues the possessor with more respect than an habitual elegant attire. Especially in the presence of the young does it add to that sense of veneration which is the chief stronghold on the affections, and enables the mother to hold her elevating sway over the impetuosity of youth. Our grandmothers studied and appreciated this matter of dress, and that they turned it to good account is verified by the fact that they are not forgotten,—they still live in their stiff brocades and ruffs. They dressed for effect, and on all occasions evinced that satisfied confidence of manner which encircles a woman who feels herself *well dressed;* for affectation arises oftener from a dissatisfied idea of not looking well, than from any desire to ape the peculiarities of another, and especially is this the case after the first bloom of youth has passed away.

The invitation "to spend the evening" was a near approach to what would now be called a party. The routine comprised a dance, that is, the solemn cotillion, for the modern "*round dance*" was considered even unchaste on the stage, and the modest "Augusta" was compelled to display the poetry of motion to admiring males alone. A song or two, "Gaily the Troubadour," "Home, Sweet Home," being chronic favorites, conversation, the last situation of the "Solitary Horseman," from the prolific pen of James, and "*refreshments handed around.*" This handing around refreshments was a most horrible invention, for it placed a diffident young man not only in a trying but in a critical position. To partake was a necessity; it would have been considered impolite to decline. The recollection of the ordeal is frightful even now. One hand was occupied in steadying a cup of boiling hot tea or coffee, the other required to firmly grasp a plate piled with cake and sweetmeats, while close beside the bewildered beau sat a demure demoiselle expecting to be entertained with a limpid flow of conversation. To sip the steaming fluid without spilling a drop was something of a task; but to accomplish the feat while intently watching the plate of liquid sweets, lest by an unlucky slant the contents should glide to trowsers and thence flow over the best Brussels, required a dexterity and a nerve which would reflect credit on the most expert juggler. The climax was reached when, as was frequently the case, the eye of a doting parent was scrutinizing every movement with an all-absorbing interest. The fearful performance seemed interminable ere one was relieved by the servant, who under instructions smilingly inquired if you would be helped to another half hour of mental and physical discomfort. "No, I thank you; nothing more," was uttered in all sincerity accompanied by an inward prayer of thankfulness that the evening was spent without positive disaster.

A writer in *Putnam's Monthly* has discoursed eloquently on the magnificent entertainments given in the manor houses of New York; at the Walton House, the Kipp Mansion, etc, in Dutch and Colonial times. He mentions the display of massive family silver emblazoned with coats of arms, and says an expensive and elegant style of living began already take place in New York. He notes a *recherché* breakfast given to John Adams when on his way through the city to attend the first Congress and describes how the simple New Englander was struck by the opulence which met his eye in every direction, and yet the same authority says: "it is evident from his (Adams') journal that he saw little of the best society, as he was entertained by two lawyers who had grown wealthy by their profession; in other words, they were *nouveau riche*." The representatives of British power doubtless brought over with them the evidences of wealth and the appliances of aristocratic luxury, and their style of living may have been imitated by a few of the Dutch Burghers, but they were exceptions, and if dinner parties were fashionable among them, the custom was very moderately followed by their Knickerbocker descendants. There were a few gentlemen of Knickerbocker parentage who prided themselves on their dinners; *bon vivants* who had cooks that understood how many turns of the spit were required to present a canvas back duck or a partridge in the highest possible perfection. Men who had educated their tastes to the nicest point in Sherries, Ports, Madeiras and Clarets, who appreciated the witching hour of twilight, when the business of the day was ended, with inside shutters closed and curtains drawn to exclude the bustle of the outer world, they could in the society of some chosen companions smack their lips over a variety of well served dainties. "But one swallow does not make Summer." Knickerbocker life was too stable, too uniform to countenance stag dinner parties, when the consequent orgies would run far into the night. That would have been a blur upon the home of the "*gute frau*" under no circumstances to be permitted, and there would have been precious little enjoyment in a set noon repast, which would have to be hurried through to enable the participants to return to the drudgery of daily toil. The Yankee Thanksgiving, with its turkey, cranberry sauce, mince, pumpkin, apple pie and cider, found favor with the dames of Knickerbocker proclivities, who not to be outdone, had added the indigestible doughnut and cruller to the dyspepsia provoking list. But these grand dinners were only informal family gatherings representative of all the living generations, including the puling babe,—the more the merrier,—at which every one present was expected to outeat himself, and only to retire from the table when compelled by actual surfeit. An invitation to dinner was not a rare occurrence; it however merely signified that the guest was welcome to partake of an abundant but simple repast, in nine cases out of ten void of display, and rarely any attempt at ostentation.

Society under Knickerbocker rule was based on a strict observance of moderation in everything. It was a *stickler* for systematic routine; it exacted respect for public opinion in every minute particular; it required the punctilious observance of its mandate at home and abroad; it deemed that it was proper to attend a stated place of worship on the Sabbath; it held that to frequent certain places was wrong; it looked with abhorrence upon the spendthrift; it condemned the idler; it believed in a straight and narrow path of duty to your fellow man; it aided and encouraged honest industry; its pride was an honored home.

New York did not become a dancing city until the advent of the Teutonic horde. When the German element became strong, the *Garden*, the *Dance*, the *Song*, with the accompanying "Lager" were introduced into every day life, and these rapidly broke through the barricades with which Dutch dignity and New England Puritanism had encircled society.

Up to the period of this influx from "*Vaterland*," Tammany Hall and the Apollo Saloon more than sufficed to meet the terpsichorean demand, which was limited by the annual balls given by fire companies, military organizations, and some few political clubs, who adopted this method to replenish their respective treasuries. Tammany Hall was the chosen salon of the fire-laddies of the old regime; during the winter months they congregated there with their dulcineas and held high carnival in their own peculiar manner.

This volunteer fire department is not understood at the present day, for tradition brands it as a band of dangerous outlaws, who preyed upon the city unrestrained by discipline or moral force. When the organization was in its prime its roll of membership embraced some sixteen hundred names, among which could be found some of the most promising young and middle aged men of the city, who entered into their duties with a zeal which bordered on infatuation. The rivalry that existed inspired them to deeds of daring and valor. Efficient promptness was the aim, and to that is due the world-wide reputation accorded to the New York firemen for the vim with which they performed their perilous and arduous tasks. The majority of the force was made up of hardy mechanics, who when their toil for the day was over, made the engine house a rendezvous to chat over the last *run*, rub up and polish the pet machine, but above all to be in readiness to respond with a will to the first stroke of the City Hall bell. In the meantime they were well behaved, orderly citizens; strong, active, full of fun and frolic, ready for a race, and if need be a tussle, but very far from being plunderers or rowdies in the modern sense. Some companies were more exclusive than others, better educated and more refined, owing to their neighboring associates, but there was an "*esprit du corps*" pervading the whole mass which acted as a check against open lawlessness and insubordination. The engineers and the majority of the foremen were well-known, responsible and respectable citizens. John Riker, James Gulick, A. B. Purdy, Elijah F. Lewis, Edward Hotimire, Allen R. Jollie, Edward Blanchard, Carlisle Norwood, Sherman Brownell, the gay Harry Howard, A. F. Pentz, F. R. Lee, Isaac L. Varian, Harmon Westervelt, James H. Titus and hosts of others were efficient officers of the department, and prominent directors in the most responsible insurance companies on Manhattan Island. The trouble lay in the fact that the outside public did not separate the sheep from the goats; each engine house was beset and disgraced by a crowd of idle hangers-on, who either begged, borrowed or stole a fire cap and coat, and who during a conflagration or a race to reach the scene, pressed into the ranks, and committed depredations or acts of violence which reflected seriously upon the whole organization, which was not only expected to do its whole duty in subduing a conflagration but also to act as police and preserve the public peace. A considerable element in the department was composed of a class known as "Bowery boys," peculiar in dress, gait, manner, tone; an inimitable species of the race, attempted for some time to be copied on the stage, but the portraiture was either so weak or so grossly exaggerated as scarcely to be recognized. These "B'hoys" had fashions of their own, which they adhered to with all the tenacity of a reigning belle; they were the most consummate dandies of the day, though they affected to look upon a Broadway swell with most decided contempt. The hair of the b'hoy or fire laddie was one of his chief cares, and from appearance the engrossing object of his solicitude. At the back of the head it was cropped as close as scissors could cut, while the front locks permitted to grow to considerable length were matted by a lavish application of *bears grease*, the ends tucked under so as to form a roll, and brushed until they shone like glass bottles. His broad, massive face, was closely shaven, as beards in any shape were deemed effeminate, and so forbidden by their creed; a black, straight, broad-brimmed hat, polished as highly as a hot iron could effect, was worn with a pitch forward, with a slight inclination to one side, intended to impart a rakish air; a large shirt collar turned down and loosely fastened, school boy fashion, so as to expose the full proportions of a thick, brawny neck; a black frock coat with skirts extending below the knee; a flashy satin or velvet vest, cut so low as to display the entire bosom of a shirt, often embroidered; pantaloons tight to the knee, thence gradually swelling in size to the bottom, so as nearly to conceal a foot usually of most ample dimensions. This stunning make-up was heightened by a profusion of jewelry as varied and costly as the b'hoy could procure. His rolling swaggering gait on the promenade on the Bowery; his position, at rest, reclining against a lamp or awning post; the precise angle of the ever-present cigar; the tone of voice, something between a falsetto and a growl; the unwritten slang which constituted his vocabulary cannot be described; even the talented Chanfrau, after devoted study of the *role*, failed to come up to the full reality in his popular and much admired delineation of *Mose*.

The b'hoys female friend, whether wife, sister or sweetheart, was as odd and eccentric as her curious protector. Her style of attire was a cheap but always greatly exaggerated copy of the prevailing Broadway mode; her skirt was shorter and fuller; her bodice longer and lower; her hat more flaring and more gaudily trimmed; her handkerchief more ample and more flauntingly carried; her corkscrew curls thinner, longer and stiffer, but her gait and swing were studied imitations of her lord and master, and she tripped by the side of her beau ideal with an air which plainly said "I know no fear and ask no favor."

Running with his favorite machine or sauntering on the Bowery the fire-laddie was a most interesting study to the naturalist, but on the ball-room floor at Tammany he was "seen, felt and understood," unapproachable, "alone in his glory." The b'hoy danced; to dance he required space. "No pent up Utica, etc.," for his every movement was widespread as the swoop of the American eagle, which, by-the-bye, was his favorite bird; the symbol of his patriotism; its effigy was the crowning glory of his darling engine. Each cotillion was opened by a bow to his partner and another to the lady on the right. This bow, composed of a twitch, a jerk and a profound salaam, was an affair so grand, so complicated, that to witness it amply repaid a somewhat dangerous visit to one of their festive gatherings. It behooved, however, the outside visitor to be very cautious and undemonstrative while gratifying his curiosity, for the laddies were proud, jealous of intruders; they would not brook the slightest approach to a sneer or unseemly stare; but, above all, the Broadway exquisite who ventured "within the pale" was compelled to be very guarded in his advances towards any fair one whose peculiar style he might chance for the moment to admire. These gaily caparisoned ladies were closely watched by their muscular admirers, and any approach to familiarity either by word or look was certain to be visited by instant punishment of a positive nature.

The pistol and knife now used by the modern cowardly bravado were not then in vogue, but these formidable *braves* carried fists backed by muscle, which were powerful weapons for aggressive purposes. As the ball progressed these active, independent citizens warmed to their work, and when coats became oppressive and burthensome, they were, *sans ceremonie*, thrown aside, and the exercises continued in shirt sleeves of bright red flannel. Most of the b'hoys wore *dickeys*, an almost irreconcilable deception, but accounted for by the fact that the red flannel shirt was the prominent article of his uniform. It was always donned that he might be prepared for the magic cry of "fire! fire! turn out! turn out!" for at the welcome sound he bounded like a deer from awning-post, work-shop or ball-room. Besides this red garment was his hobby; on its front the number of his company was conspicuously displayed in muslin figures as a general rule, but occasionally embroidered by the hand of his lady love in the most elaborate style. These magic numerals fixed his identity beyond a doubt, and each was feared or respected in proportion to the strength of the particular clan in which he was enrolled. These boys were eminently clannish, and on a given signal they rallied for defence or assault, without special enquiry as to the cause of action or whether the scene of conflict was on a street corner or in the ball-room surrounded by their respective goddesses.

Many years ago when the Tammany Hall ball-room was in its full bloom, a verdant youth fired by an insane idea to see life in all its phases, resolved to visit the famous rendezvous on a certain evening selected by a crack fire company for their annual ball. Dressed in the trimmest Broadway cut, swallow tail, straps, high choker and all, he entered the door, paid his dollar, and then sauntered in among the unterrified, expecting to create no slight sensation in the ranks of the assembled belles of the Eastern District by his elaborate make-up. He was not wrong as to his surmise in regard to sensation, but his premises were not accurately taken. A red flag is not more efficacious in exciting the ire of a Spanish bull than was the rig of a Broadv v dandy to arouse the pugnacious tendencies of *Mose* or his ally *Syksie*, and especially when the much despised *th g* intruded itself upon their own stamping ground in the presence of *Lize* trigged out in full regalia. Mose watched with cat like eye the innocent youth who lolled from place to place, casting furtive glances hither and thither in the hope of meeting the gaze of some damsel more plucky than himself who would ask him to join in a festive cotillion. No one, however, of the dashing houri's took compassion on the bashful stranger as dance after dance was called by Monsieur De Grand Valle, the acknowledged ballet master, and who had been from the earliest recollection of the oldest inhabitant the dancing professor in that special locality, and whether he is still "*chasséeing*" in his round-toed pumps as merrily as ever, "*Quien Sabé.*" It would have been well for the self invited stranger if he had retired with disgust at the lack of courtesy on the part of managers and the assembled company. He did quit the fascinating scene several times, but only to return to the charge fortified by stimulants imbibed for the purpose of rallying his nerve. In due time the ardent produced the desired effect; his courage mounted to the proper standard to meet even the risk of a decided refusal, and he boldly requested the most timid wall flower he could select to honor him with her hand for the ensuing dance. The coy damsel complied with apparent willingness, and the pair were soon gliding through the intricacies of "balance to your partner" and "forward two." The jig was soon over, and the courageous swain escorted his fascinating partner to her seat, overjoyed at his success, resolving in his mind whether it would not be manly to do the thing over again, and then invite her to the supper-room as a finishing stroke of gallantry. "*L'homme propose; Dieu dispose.*" The adventurous hero had scarcely time to make his obeisance when he found himself tossed to and fro, as the dry leaf is whirled by the wintry blast. The cause of this sudden tumult no one deigned to tell. "Hustle him out!" was obeyed by as many red shirts as could possibly assist in the operation, and the imperative operation was executed as rapidly as the dense crowd would allow. The door having been passed the scared youth was seized by the neck with a powerful grip and hurried to the stairs leading to the floor below, which he soon reached through the impetus imparted by a well directed kick, when he picked up his considerably rumpled person amid the jeers and taunts of his tormentors. Under such circumstances home was the much desired goal, and before retiring to rest, in conning over the disastrous events, and in taking account of the profit and loss of the adventure, the youthful traveller "in ways that are dark" found that he had left one skirt of his swallow-tail in the possession of the enemy, but, *per contra*, no bones were broken, no reporters present, so the trifling loss was carried to experience account, which all young men should carefully keep for reference, not for the purpose of advising younger brothers, but to profit by the entries there noted down.

The Apollo Ball Room on the east side of Broadway near the junction of Canal Street was a far more pretentious saloon than Tammany. Being on Broadway there was a marked mixture of classes, and candor compels the admission that "calico and check apron" was the prevailing type so far as the female patrons were concerned, while the male element can safely be classed as democratic. It was not deemed *proper* that those who wished to be considered ladies and gentlemen should be present at public balls; so in consequence of this provision in the Knickerbocker statutes, fashionable Young America was compelled to be extremely cautious lest his visits to the Apollo be discovered in aristocratic circles; but, above all, that they eluded the argus eyes of the powers at home, who not only were responsible for his morals but controlled the purse strings, and would surely for such a breach of decorum cut off the supply of dollars in a most summary way. But love has always laughed at bolts and bars; so love of fun and frolic inspired staid Knickerbocker youths to break through stringent rules to take the chances, and as fruits of disobedience they enjoyed many a lively dance, with lots of nice flirtations in the society of cheerful, bright-eyed milliners and dress-makers who hailed from the classic region of Division Street, not reared under the strict code which governed west of Broadway.

For the life of them these New York grisettes could see no possible harm in the society of a juvenile exquisite who became wild with the idea that he was indulging in contraband pleasure. The innocent and fascinating creatures enjoyed listening to the recital of the schemes necessary to compass the undertaking; they laughed boisterously about the duplicate basement key, procured at the greatest possible risk, with only Betty or Dinah in the secret, by means of which the "pattern" who was supposed to be peacefully slumbering under the parental roof, could slip in ere his doting parents were astir. The boy in turn was carried away by so much sympathetic interest and longed for the time to pass when they could meet again and talk over fresh difficulties surmounted. Such reminiscences will bring back the Old Apollo to many a man whose dancing days are over, who can recall the substantial iron key which had to be so carefully inserted, so daintily turned, lest the slightest noise should lead to detection; how closely he clung to the baluster to avoid any tell tale creak; how he held his breath while passing the front bed-room door; how nervously he listened when his own apartment was reached, to be surely satisfied that all was thus far safe; but, above all, will he remember the painful sense of relief he experienced when breakfast was over, and no doubtful questions had been proposed from either the head or the foot of the table and Betty had proved faithful and not snickered or looked wise.

One Winter a bold attempt was made to overturn the established law. Young America in solemn conclave resolved to dance openly and above board, if possible, and to do away with underground fun and frolic. To compass that end, to leave nothing undone, to obtain parental acquiesence by honorable means, to merit the approbation of *mamas* and perchance gain the active support of the leaders in society, though it was well understood the movement would meet with determined opposition from dominie and elder, who looked upon the dance as sinful in itself, besides being a waste of time which should be devoted to higher and nobler purposes; for these worthies carried their views on the subject so far that they would rise and leave a little coterie gathered in a family parlor if the young people ventured to form a cotillion in their presence. In spite, however, of this antagonistic element, the Ladies Dining Room of the City Hotel was secured for the purpose of giving a series of sociables, at which none but subscribers, and those the *crème de la crème*, should be admitted. Tickets, limited in number, positively not transferrable, and at the then exhorbitant figure of twenty-five dollars for the series of five, were issued. A committee of men, well known to be good and true, was chosen as arbitrary managers, with full power to insure the most perfect decorum and propriety. John Charruaud was selected as general supervisor and floor manager, and as he had taught the grandmothers, mothers and daughters of the city all the poetry of motion which Gotham then could boast of, that choice left no room for cavil. The City Hotel reunions were pronounced a success. Many noted beauties of the day honored them with their presence and the company was admitted to be as select as though congregated in a private parlor by special invitation. Still, notwithstanding all the precautions taken, the admitted fact that every detail was *comme il faut*, that nothing occurred which could possibly wound the most sensitive, New York was not yet prepared to endorse the threatened inroad on the established idea of female seclusiveness. The old time dowagers, backed by the minister, denounced the sociables, pronounced them a breach of decorum, tossed their caps and emphasized "*indelicate*" when the names of some fair ones chanced to be mentioned in their presence, who had patronized these efforts to enhance social life and innocent enjoyment. The battle for supremacy was bravely waged on both sides, but the old ladies beat Young America and the City Hotel sociables were discontinued. Under such circumstances what was male Young America, out of his teens, to do? He had discovered that the Tammanyites were by far too pugnacious, too set in their peculiar views for comfort, that Charruaud's monthly gatherings were little else than school exhibitions, gotten up to tickle the *amour propre* of doting mothers, invariably present to be assured that no mirth should meddle with the serious, smileless business of the decorous cotillion,—so staid, that Charlie, Dick or Tom were forced to "cut their pigeon wings" with theological sobriety; any juvenile antic which might cause a faint glimmer to light up the placid features of Mary Jane or Catharine Ann, was sure to be detected by the watchful Minervas, and the thoughtless little belles were frowned on as a punishment for their levity. So perforce as a last resource to find some vent for the love of sport that was in us, we were driven to the Apollo to enjoy a rollicking dance, free from unnatural restraints of unyielding formality, but always kept within proper bounds by that civility which regulates American assemblages where woman is present.

CHAPTER THIRTEENTH.

"Let the players be well used; for they are the abstracts and brief chronicles of the times; after your death you were better have a bad epitaph, than their ill report while you live.—*Hamlet.*

There were four theatres in the city, *i. e.*, the Park, American (now Bowery), Franklin, and Richmond Hill. The Park, situated on Park Row, between Ann and Beekman Streets, was erected in 1798, but was burnt and rebuilt in 1821, and was calculated to contain about 2,500 persons when filled to its utmost capacity. Under the management of Simpson and Price it was the acknowledged histrionic temple not only of New York but of the United States. A successful engagement played on its stage, served as the "*open sesame*" to all others in the country, and a hearty endorsement by Park audiences operated as a sure quietus to rural criticism, not excepting Boston. The architecture of the building could not be classed under the head of any known order; it simply presented to the eye a wall front of bricks and plaster with windows and doors pierced here and there as convenience or circumstance dictated; it might have been taken for a barrack, store-house or Methodist meeting, had it not been for a statue representing the "Bard of Avon," thoughtfully placed over the main entrance to proclaim its special dedication to the Muses. Its interior arrangements, decorations and appointments will appear niggardly and mean, perhaps ridiculous, by contrast with the palatial homes of the drama now reared in every section of the city, in the decoration and embellishment of which such vast sums are annually expended to satisfy the taste for luxury characteristic of the present hour. The entrances to the Park were narrow and dingy, the lobbies uncarpeted and dark; for the source of light, an oil lamp, was not calculated to produce a dazzling effect. Brilliant illumination, however, was not requisite to display elaborate frescoes, choice marbles or artistic mouldings; the old Park lobbies were as plain as the trowel and saw could make them. The walls were tinted first one color and then another with apparently no other object or aim than to hide dirt, and vary the monotony; so the primitive tools used to rejuvenate and redecorate the temple were the scrubbing brush and the white, yellow or blue-wash brush, while the artists employed were good old darkies who did their work faithfully for the consideration of six shillings per diem. The auditorium consisted of three tiers of boxes and the *Pit*. The settees of the first and second tier were furnished with backs and the seats covered with dark moreen, an article pronounced everlasting and warranted not to fade; they were narrow, straight and hard, so it required good acting to enable one to sit out a performance. The pit was occupied exclusively by the sterner sex, and was reached by a narrow subterranean passage, admirably planned to suit the operations of pickpockets, for two abreast stopped the way. Its furniture consisted of long, unbacked, stationary benches, uncushioned and roughly-planed at that, with barely room between to crowd by, to say nothing of any possible extensions of limb. Such accommodations offered no attractions to the gentler sex, whose descendants in the female line now pay extra prices to lounge on the cushioned chairs of the aristocratic parquette, and on the sofas of the choice orchestra stalls, for they have lately discovered that this formerly-despised pit was the spot not only to see and hear, but also to be seen. The Park pit was not the *hi, hi,* place which many may picture it, and it must not be associated with the peanuts and slang which are so apt to be linked with its name. It was no bar to respectability to be seen there, that is to say, by those who were seated in the boxes; for to frequent the theatre at all was deemed sinful by a large and influential class of citizens. The pit ruled the judgment of the house, for the critics and reporters congregated there and the actor knew where the jury was seated, upon whose verdict his future on the American stage largely depended. Those jurymen as a rule were dispassionately correct, seldom permitted their decisions to be warped by prejudice or national feeling; fair play and no favor was the sentiment apt to be unanimous. One prominent exception when the old Park pit was divided it may perhaps not be amiss to relate, as upon that special occasion there was exhibited on the part of the audience a wild excitement and a riotous disposition manifested which has no parallel in the annals of the Park Theatre. Mr. and Mrs. Wood's celebrated operatic performances of the time had made one or more trips across the Atlantic and had become great favorites with New York audiences. The lady especially was not only admired as an artist of great merit, but respected by the public as a virtuous, true woman. On their passage to this country to fulfil an engagement at the Park, entered into with Mr. Price in England, they chanced to have for a fellow-passenger a New York editor, who was famous for his pugnacious tendencies. As a matter of course, on the then usual protracted voyage, people who were not affected with chronic seasickness became acquainted, so our editor and Wood proved no exceptions to the rule. On a certain day of the trip, when other topics chanced to flag, England and the United States by some accident loomed up as the subject of a discussion. Point by point the old controversies were gone over to wile away the tedious hours; but ere the *pow-wow* came to an end, both had warmed up to the importance of the issue to be then and there settled. "Rule Brittania" versus "Yankee Doodle" stood facing each other with menacing look and gesture across the narrow table; the gauntlet of war was thrown down and promptly accepted. Yankee — swore that John — should be hissed from the New York stage; John — defied these editorial slanders, and sneered at the pretended power of his wrathy adversary.

In this belligerent mood both landed and at once set about marshalling their respective forces for this trial of strength. Citizens were soon apprised of these threatened hostilities and the theatre office was besieged with eager applicants for tickets, so great was the anxiety to be present on Wood's opening night and witness the skirmishing between the high opposing parties. Despite the solicitations of the peaceful Simpson and the calm arguments of Treasurer Blake, the editorial thunderer daily vented his wrath in a leading column of his mammoth sheet, —while he lived to spill ink and use up harmless goose quills, no *British hireling* should ruffle the feathers of the American Eagle and go unwhipped. The United States Bank, the tariff, the coming election, were all for the time "dead cocks in the pit," for he had vowed the English actor should be hissed from the stage.

On the never-to-be-forgotten opening night, the house was packed from footlights to gallery. All were orderly in the dense assemblage; nothing noticeable save the unusual circumstance that there was scarcely a woman to be seen in the crowded audience. There was a buzz as the orchestra struck up the overture to the appointed opera, nothing more; and when it was concluded the pit, as was customary, awarded its accustomed quota of applause. As soon as this usual demonstration had subsided the green baize drop was slowly furled as a signal that the performance was about to commence. To describe with any accuracy the scene which followed is an impossibility. Clapping of hands, stamping of feet, accompanied by cheers, groans, hisses. Cries of "Wood! Wood!" seemed to issue simultaneously from three thousand masculine throats, and created a din which made the old shell tremble. In response to this somewhat singular, but by no means unexpected call, Wood appeared at the wing, and with an apparently firm tread walked to the footlights, but after facing the storm for a moment his confidence was shaken and he beat a hasty retreat. Mr. Simpson, the popular manager, accompanied him to the front on his second attempt, and with supplicating bow and gesture essayed to still the tumult. He displayed a placard which announced that he and Mr. Wood desired to be heard in their defense; but manager, Wood and placard were forced to retire without effecting their object. Still the yells were continuous, but the curtain was not lowered as a signal of defeat. Wood was not willing to abandon the field to his adversary without one more attempt. He again strode with marked determination to the footlights, but was not only received with a volley of unearthly yells; missiles were hurled at him by the habitues of the third tier. Then ensued a scene which perhaps has often been described in sensation novels, but one which is seldom enacted in every-day life, and witnessed by thousands of spectators. So soon as this new danger presented itself Mrs. Wood rushed to the front and threw her woman's form between her husband and his assailants. The effect produced by the sudden movement on her part was electrical. Such ringing cheers as greeted the noble woman never before or since rang within the walls of a theatre, and the *pitites* of the Old Park gave her round after round of applause with a vim which drowned the continued hisses of the *gods* and soon deterred them from further attempts at bodily harm. The pit had been divided by prejudice for and against Wood, but that sentiment quickly vanished when the self sacrificing wife tearfully pleaded for mercy in behalf of her rash and hot-headed husband.

Far from being an educated musician, the writer feels that he cannot do full justice to the talented orchestra of the Park; no special wrong, however, can be committed by endeavoring, after the lapse of years, to describe a select number of worthy men, who night after night were punctually at their posts, and delighted us with choice selections from the "Bronze Horse" or accompanied Chapman with accepted skill, when he thrilled his auditors with the pathetic ballad entitled the "Teetotal Society."

The leader of the band was seated a very trifle above his subordinates; he did not wield a magic *baton* and swing it wildly about, as is the habit of modern conductors; neither did he wriggle and twist, but looked straight ahead, fiddled right along from page to page, until the little bell told him to stop. His repertoire was not extensive, but satisfied the popular craving; old acquaintances in music, as well as in everything else, were welcome, and he would always answer an encore without going through the ceremony of bowing right and left, and save himself the trouble of placing his hand upon the supposed region of his impulsive, artistic heart. The violin of the leader was sustained by a flute, cornet, trombone, bass viol, violincello, clarionet, cymbals and *drums*, all common instruments, all save one played on by ordinary men, and that one the man who officiated during many years in the *drum* department, which was located in the left hand corner of the orchestra. The operator on the two drums was a character who beyond a doubt opened his eyes in London, for Cockney was unmistakably stamped around and about his dumpy person from top to toe. His patronymic not having been handed down, it is most fitting that he should hereafter be known as Mr. Drum. Drum was short and stout, his large round head was bald and shining at the top, his eyes were small and inclined to be watery, his apoplectic face was closely shaven, his nose was stubby and highly colored, his mouth made to fit any pewter mug manufactured. A black silk stock occupied the narrow space between his ears and shoulders, where it was met by the glazed collar of a snuff-brown coat which enveloped his barrel-shaped body to the point at which it was hidden from the public gaze by the formidable instruments upon which it was his nightly duty to hammer most unmercifully. Drum must have been the possessor of a wonderful memory, so far as drum music was concerned, for if he used notes they were never exposed, but like those of extempore preachers, artistically concealed. During his rests he was the impersonation of lethargy; he sat on his stool with closed eyes, apparently dead to all surroundings; but, when time was called, he delivered his well directed blows with a will, which compelled the trombone man to put forth every human effort that the concord of sweet sounds might be maintained. When the leader favored us with the overture to the Bronze Horse, Drum seemed to wake from his stupor as if fully aware that the main success of that grand composition depended upon the free exercise of his wonderful beating powers. Wind and string instruments were nowhere in the struggle when he was surely aroused. Drum had a "full hand," he "played it alone," and would never have tired had not his well-trained ear caught the tinkle of that little bell hidden somewhere in the depths below, when down fell the sticks, and the man of energy sank back motionless until again called into action by the tiny monitor behind the green baize curtain.

From the prominence given to Mr. Drum it must not be inferred that the Park orchestra was destitute of real musical talent, for hundreds will not fail to recall one of its number, Alexander Kyle, who for years was the champion flute player in America, and many are doubtless living who time and again honored him with a hearty encore when a solo on that instrument chanced to be a feature of the musical entertainment.

The patrons of the Park were fond of English Opera, and were occasionally favored even when no foreign singing-bird of high repute was available. Cinderella long held the front rank in popular favor, and was produced by the stock companies without the aid of any particular star. On such occasions Mrs. Austin, a pretty, pert actress, with a sweet voice of no inconsiderable cultivation, was the Prima Donna. Mr. Jones, the standing tenor of the company, sang the role of the *Prince* very acceptably. Jones was a singing-master but no actor, while Harry Placide, a great actor but no vocalist, was the *Baron Pumpolino* on all occasions. William F Brough was for a considerable period attached to the Park as a singing member, and was always so complaisant as to indulge the musical critics of the pit by favoring them with "The Wolf." This famous ballad was so intensely guttural in tone that it called into requisition the full power of the trombone as a fitting accompaniment in those lower depths reached by the powerful organ of the great basso profundo. Opera was, however, the exception in the varied list of entertainment at the Park.

Stars of the first theatrical magnitude were engaged in the London market, many of whom met with such success as to frequently repeat their visits, while some among them never returned to their native country. Among the first mentioned occur the names of Cooke, Young, Edmund Kean, Charles Kemble, Tyrone Power, Sinclair, Miss Ellen Tree, Fanny Kemble, with lesser luminaries, who in turn appeared; while Cooper, Junius Brutus Booth, Vandenhoff, J. W. Wallack, John and Charles Mason were among the stars who fancied our semi-barbarous manners and customs and settled among the Yankees.

It was, however, in the stock company attached to the Park that our interest centered, for it was to that we were indebted for our real theatrical treats.

In a troupe where all were fixed stars, differing only in degree of excellence, but unsurpassed at the time in their several specialties; who have played together on the same stage for so long a period, that they appeared more like a family group congregated for their own amusement than merely actors and actresses whose vocation was to please the public for a passing hour. It would be ungenerous to make exceptions; so far as memory serves all shall have a short notice for "auld lang syne." "*Place aux dames,*" has always been an American sentiment. Mesdames Wheatley, Vernon, Gurner, Austin, Barry, Misses Charlotte Cushman, Emma Wheatley, Clara Fisher were the much admired deities of young Gothamites, who constituted themselves their knights when the beauty or talents of these ladies were called in question by any outside barbarian who ventured upon adverse criticism.

Their judgement may have been just in the slightest degree one-sided, enthusiastic praise of this or that particular rôle, just a little strained; but their equals cannot be culled from the ranks of any company now on the New York stage.

No one of the ladies was a distinguished "*blonde;*" a *tow-head* was not the rage; high civilization had not introduced the unveiled beauties of the Black Crook school;—the "Highland Fling" in ruffled pantellettes, by a miss not far advanced in her teens proved an all-sufficient excitement, for the "Mazourka" in heavy silk skirt reaching far below the knee brought the fan into general use; caused a sudden desire for absorbing conversation, and the *danseuse* was only awarded with sly, stolen glances from the boxes; no patting of tiny hands, no waving of handkerchiefs, no determined stare through powerful lorgnettes, no smiles of wild delight when her artistic display was ended. This timidity on the part of the ladies present may be ascribed to a squeamish affectation or to a sad lack of taste in not admiring the beauties of nature,—no matter what its cause it did exist and modesty manifested itself, and the audiences of the Old Park enjoyed a sterling comedy or drama with a hearty appetite, with a simple relish which required no doubtful spice to enhance gratification.

Mrs. Wheatley, the mother of William and Emma, was the theatrical matron, duchess and queen of the company. She was a lady of marked presence, of portly commanding figure, possessed a pleasant expressive face, an agreeable voice, always modulated to a nicety to the requirements of her assumed character, and ever perfectly at home in the varied rôles she was called upon to assume. Confident of appreciation by the audience she evidenced that composure of manner on the stage which was one of her peculiar attractions in private life. Far above mediocrity in every part assigned her, the personation of the fussy, towering dame in old English comedy was her crowning effort, and in these delineations she was never outranked during her protracted career. Fresh, cheerful, active, she seemed to keep pace with all changes, was at her post seemingly without ache or pain, and gave every outward sign that she was a century plant, and she did bloom long after the last vestige of the Park had passed away.

Death has but recently withdrawn Mrs. Vernon from the stage, and we have thus far looked in vain to catch a glimpse of a successor worthy to fill her place on the boards. The present generation have too often applauded, nay cheered the genial, mirth-provoking old lady to need any reminder of her unsurpassed ability in a line of character which she early appropriated and to which she uninterruptedly clung during the more than half century of her theatrical life. The Fisher family, from which she sprang, has long been noted for the marked stage ability of its members, especially in light comic roles; but, as will readily be recalled, the family was not celebrated for beauty either in the male or female line. Mrs. Vernon's portraiture of the soubrette, shrew, spicy old maid, and female Paul Pry, will ever be held in high esteem, not only by the *ancien regime*, but by the habitues of Wallack's at the present time, who had the gratification of witnessing her piquant, rollicking style, inimitable to the last, even though it had become slightly blunted by the rubs of "three score years and ten."

Mrs. Gurner, another of these favorites, did not possess the talent to soar above respectable mediocrity. Perfect in part, faultless in make up, she always was eminently satisfactory, but never astonished her most ardent admirer. Pretty, passive, retiring in manner, she looked and acted the walking lady, or dependant female relative to perfection, and if by chance absent from her well-determined sphere, the sensitive critics in the pit felt the loss of her presence and were uncomfortable.

Mrs. Barry, the stock representative widow of

dead kings and mother of murdered princes, was a large stately dame who did all the heavy business with most solemn voice and manner. How the lady would have appeared in other vesture than the sombre "habiliments of woe," or what silvery tones would have greeted the ear, had her stage lot not been cast with the dire necessity of continually cursing the crooked-backed Richard, or in uttering loud lamentations for the "untimely taking off" of her Henry and Edward, cannot even be surmised; for whenever she was in the cast the night was sure to be devoted to the performance of "deeds of dreadful note;" and as a natural consequence of her presence the orchestra was compelled to intone one or more funereal dirges. Undertakers are reported to be a cheerful, merry class when unemployed at their special calling, that being a fact Mrs. Barry may have been "a joy forever" in the domestic circle.

Charlotte Cushman, when but a mere girl, appeared on the boards of the old Park. Her slow advance in the profession was unnoticed even by those who almost nightly were present at the performance. On attaining womanhood, her development evinced nothing to arrest the attention of a casual observer. Her voice was harsh, almost masculine in quality, her manner brusque, her movements dignified and self-possessed, yet they lacked that pliant grace looked for in woman, though at times her independant dash and unwonted energy would elicit hearty bursts of applause from an audience which did not anticipate a surprise. The critics of the time noticed her performances with the greatest respect: "Miss

Cushman sustained the character of —— with her accustomed ability, showing careful study of the difficult role, etc.," but nothing more. No enthusiasm; no rapture. By degrees she imperceptibly strode to the front and was assigned leading parts in the *unavoidable absence* of some particular star who chanced to be indisposed. Still, even then the wise directors of public taste and judgement detected nothing which foretold "coming events." They praised her sprightly personation of Lady Gay Spanker, and when London Assurance was on the bills there was sure to be a paying house; but as the cast included Placide, Ritchings, Fisher, Povey, etc., Charlotte, who was the life of the piece, was only looked upon as one of a cluster of gems. So time rolled on ; her talent was tacitly admitted, but still she remained year after year at the Park, apparently a fixture, both the public and herself seemingly unconscious of the spring she was so soon to take, at one bound to become the leading actress of the English stage, and an honored guest in the highest literary circles of Europe and America. "*We all knew it !*" now cry the old time scribblers, as these worthies crowd Young Amerca aside at the entrance of Booth's magnificent dramatic temple, in their eager haste to witness once more before they die her powerful delineation of Meg Merrilies. Now when the full glare of her genius has burst upon the world and the name and fame of Charlotte Cushman is as widespread as was that of the renowned Siddons; these wiseacres remember that far back in Knickerbocker times they saw glimmerings of her great future in the artistic personation of Mrs. Haller, when at a moment's warning Miss Cushman undertook the rôle; but they do not state why they suffered her to toil on in obscurity, or why they permitted trans-Atlantic critics to herald her transcendant ability.

Emma Wheatley made her debut at the Park when only a mere child. She first appeared as a danseuse, and for a time, aided by her sister, who soon withdrew from the stage. She was the attraction between the play and the after-piece. Miss Wheatley was prepossessing in face and form; perfectly satisfactory as a dancer and posturant; modest, unassuming in manner, she pleased without ever being in any way wonderful. The long trained eye of her talented mother soon discovered that she possessed ability too decided to be wasted in a mere mechanical routine; withdrew her from the unsatisfactory rôle. Careful instruction combined with judicious training in the business of the stage, soon laid the foundation for the exalted position she attained as a delineator of the highest range of character.

Miss Wheatley was by nature excessively diffident, and at the opening of her career was by some critics pronounced too sensitive, too nervous in temperament for great success in her adopted profession; while others, among whom were Sheridan Knowles, Epes Sargeant and Fitz Green Halleck, construed her coyness and abandon of self as evidences of high art. Be that as it may, her style remained the same to the close of her theatrical career. From the beginning she was encouraged and guarded by her watchful mother, and she was invariably sustained on the stage by her brother William, who was at the time a promising young actor and attached to the stock company of the Park. Her novitiate was eminently successful. The different journals vied with each other in lauding her Desdemona, Julia, Mrs. Haller Mrs. Beverly, &c., and she was fast gathering histrionic garlands when she was snatched from the stage by a marriage with a fine representative of Young America named James Mason, the scion of a wealthy family of New York, whose father, John Mason, was the then President of the Chemical Bank.

Ere the nuptual knot was tied, the young favorite bade adieu to the stage at a complimentary benefit tendered her in the New National Theatre, on the corner of Leonard and Church streets. Othello was selected as the play, and the cast of that evening has never been surpassed, if it has been equalled, on the stage. Edwin Forrest, then in his zenith, appeared as the jealous Moor, the great Booth was *the* Iago, James W. Wallack played Cassio, William Wheatley enacted Roderigo, Mrs. Sefton was the Emilia, while the "beneficiare," in her happiest vein delineated the gentle Desdemona. The house was crammed; the audience electrified by the efforts of this galaxy of talent. Each star was greeted with round upon round of applause, and when the curtain fell, all were vociferously called to the footlights to receive a parting ovation. When the curtain was drawn up in response to the popular demand, the quick eyes in the pit discovered that one planet, *or rather one comet*, was missing from the group, and sudden as thought the cry of Booth! Booth! rang through the theatre. The Iago of the night did not appear, and the clamor became more intense, but after a few moments of continuous uproar the popular, erratic genius, already half disrobed, calmly stepped forward to satisfy his determined admirers. After making the customary obeisance he did not at once retire, but stood like a statue as if bewildered by the storm of excited cheers with which he was greeted. A speech! a speech! instantly produced death-like silence as if by magic; the attitude, expression, manner of the unapproached actor can only be pictured by those who are so fortunate as to have witnessed his marvellous magnetic powers. He seemed riveted to the spot when he realized the position in which he had placed himself by his momentary abstraction; his flashing eye glanced from pit to dome in an instant, his foot moved as it was wont to do when Richard whispers "I wish the bastards dead; and I would have it suddenly performed," as he responded in a clear, ringing, but somewhat sarcastic tone, "Ladies and gentlemen, if you are satisfied, *I am*," and then retired amid cheers and peals of boisterous laughter.

Young and Old America saw Emma Wheatley withdraw from the stage with many a deep drawn sigh, feeling assured that they would not soon "look upon her like again."

Mrs. Mason, however, did not long enjoy the seclusion of private life. The alliance was distasteful to the family of her husband, and she was too proud to make any advances tending to conciliation, and soon all intercourse ceased, and the door of his former home was barred against him; but he was a favorite with his father, and during the life of the latter the young couple were provided with the necessaries for subsistence. John Mason, full of years, sickened and died, when James found himself penniless and disinherited. He was one of the few young men of New York who had been reared in luxury; his education was as refined and elegant as money could secure, but with no aim at practical utility; in a word, he was an accomplished gentleman, had grown to manhood without profession or trade, which was then, and is in a great measure now, a certain bar against the possibility of earning a livlihood. He had no business tact or knowledge, no business circle or acquaintance, and as a sequence was as helpless as a child.

Mrs. Mason, like a true woman, did not hesitate a moment; they needed money to sustain life, but above all he needed ample means to contest his father's will, which he was satisfied would be set aside when properly presented to the legal tribunals. Terms were soon made with Mr. Simpson and her return to the boards was greeted by enthusiastic audiences. The suit was commenced; both denied themselves everything not absolutely needed so that the means should be in hand to aid the restoration of the husband's rights in his father's immense estate, and the faithful wife toiled on, generously patronized by the public, until the desired end was accomplished and her husband was awarded his unjustly withheld fortune. The goal reached, Mrs.

Mason at once withdrew from the stage with increased reputation as a finished actress accompanied by unfeigned respect as a noble woman.

One who knew them well can testify how cheerfully they bore their protracted doubts, privations, and at times actual suffering; but he also had the privilege of being a sharer in their bright, childlike anticipations when the clouds of adversity seemed to have been dispersed. He can vividly recall their unaffected merriment when scene after scene of discomfort through which they had passed was recounted in the cosy parlor of their unostentatious country home, surrounded by the few friends who had cheered them in their dark hours, and who rejoiced with them in the prospect of ease and luxury, which, so far as mortal eye could discern, was decreed to be their future lot in life. But sad to relate, ere the first blush of prosperity had faded, in the full bloom of personal and mental charms, surrounded by all the appliances that taste and devotion could invent to please her refined nature, Mrs. Mason was suddenly summoned to bid farewell to the man she so fondly loved and for whom she had so faithfully, so persistently struggled.

Clara Fisher, afterwards Mrs. Maeder, was a niece of Mrs. Vernon. She appeared at the Park as a "Youthful Prodigy," and inherited in a remarkable degree the talent of her noted family. She selected for her début the character of "Little Pickle" in the farce entitled "The Spoiled Child." She was precocious; became a marked favorite; was applauded, petted, praised without limit, and soon became a spoiled child in reality;

so far as any marked improvement could be discerned. Her early smartness did not keep pace with her years, and as is often the case, the wonderful infant did not culminate in an extraordinary woman. She glided almost imperceptibly from the stage, but was long known as a cultivated musician and highly esteemed as a teacher.

Harry Placide, but lately deceased, at a ripe old age, was beyond a doubt the most brilliant general actor of his day. He was always acceptable to his audience, besides being a man in whom the manager could place perfect confidence. His rare talent was not limited by any specialty, it ranged from grave to gay, from Grandfather Whitehead to the fat schoolboy, whose delights lay in trundling hoops and eating gingerbread

During his long continuous career on the boards of one theatre he was not surpassed in his conception and depiction of the refined, courtly gentleman, either of the old or new school, they were studies one never tired in witnessing. For such portraitures his physique was singularly adapted. His person was very attractive; his features refined and elegant when in repose, yet unusually expressive; his manners easy and graceful; his voice soft yet manly in its modulation and tone.

Perfectly "au fait" by early education and study in all the details which distinguish a polished man of the world, he walked the stage and entered into his assumes character without any of those conventional *stagey* mannerisms which often mar the performances of men who claim to be stars of the first theatrical degree. Many of these stars never lose sight of themselves, their self-importance is absolutely appalling, it perceptibly looms through every garb, through every character they assume, and the careful observer will see the well-known form and figure of the famous tragedian Smith undimmed alike by gloomy Hamlet, crafty Richelieu, ambitious Richard, trusting Othello, conniving Iago, or Sir Giles Overreach, or Sir Edward Mortimer; in fine, the whole repertoire through which Mr. Smith "struts his brief hour upon the stage." If Placide was a victim of this inordinate vanity, he possessed the happy faculty of showing it only at rare intervals, when he played the part of Henry Placide in private circles. Sir Peter Teazle, Sir Harcourt Courtley, Baron Pompolino, and Grandfather Whitehead were in his hands gems of acting worth miles of travel to witness. In low comedy and farce he brought to bear all the humor needful to a decided hit, but never forgot himself or his audience by being unmindful of Hamlet's advice to the players. Tyrone Power, the acknowledged Irishman of the stage, who unfortunately has had no successor as yet worthy to wear the mantle of his fame, was a generous, appreciative man, and possessed a keen sense of the ridiculous. During his several engagements at the Park he was supported in many of his characters by Placide, one of which is especially remembered. In this play Placide was assigned the part of a phlegmatic Dutchman, between whom and the rollicking Irishman a most unaccountable intimacy springs up, and the odd twain are supposed to be traveling in company through Ireland. In many scenes of this play Power seemed to forget himself and joined the audience in their applause and laughter, as Placide growled and grumbled at the misery and discomfort which met him at every turn during his sojourn in the Emerald Isle. One scene in particular is recalled when the agonized Dutchman, with horror-stricken tones exclaims, "Mein Gott, vat a kountree, vat a beebles." The attitude, the look of despair, the gutteral, mournful tone of Placide, were so supremely ridiculous that the great Power lost all self control, and for a time was convulsed with unaffected, genuine laughter. No comedian ever received a higher meed of praise.

It is the general belief that actors as a rule are he most selfish of mortals; that they are the most censorious critics of each other; that jealousy forms a preponderant ingredient of stage life. An incident at the Park may prove interesting as an illustration that great actors can be generous and at times impulsive in the praise of a rival. The first appearance of Charles Kean at the Park theatre, on the boards where his father in former years had electrified New York audiences, was anticipated as an uncommon theatrical event. For days preceding his opening expectation was rife, great things were hoped for from the son of the renowned Edmund; so the house was filled with the refined and educated patrons of the drama. Young Kean had chosen Richard, a character in which his renowned sire shone the brightest, both in England and America. In the rendition and acting of this thrilling rôle the elder

Kean had powerful competitors, so powerful that the partizan spirit engendered almost culminated in a riot at the rival houses of Drury Lane and Covent Garden. Foremost among the ambitious disputants to become the acknowledged Roscius, was Junius Brutus Booth, whose ardent admirers claimed for him the much-coveted crown; but especially did they boldly assert that he stood alone and unapproached in his delineation of the Duke of Gloster. Certain it was that in this country through long years Booth was the standard Richard of the American stage; by his standard all aspirants have been criticized, and equally certain it is that no one of the many who have appeared could invest the villainous character with that fearful reality and painful interest which characterized his personation of the rôle. His physique, his nervous temperament, his restless eye, his reckless manner, his consummate bye-play, his devilish sneer, found full scope in the different scenes presented by the play and he seemed fitted as it were by nature to portray to the life Shakespeare's ideal monster.

This Junius Brutus Booth was among the assemblage congregated to welcome and to pass judgment upon the young Kean on his first appearance at the Park. He was doubtless a close observer as the son of his great rival passed through an ordeal which was to make or mar his fortunes in the new world. Charles Kean was a wonderful actor; more than wonderful when his glaring physical defects are considered; more wonderful still for the tact he displayed not only in concealing them, but at times in converting them into actual beauties. His figure was short and disproportioned, yet his action on the stage was smooth, always commanding, and at times graceful; his voice was harsh and singularly uneven, his occasional hesitancy of speech almost amounted to a decided stammer; still, by the aid of his powerful will he so mesmerized his auditors that the broken articulation ceased to grate upon the ear, and his hereditary genius, by which he was enabled to overcome barriers apparently insurmountable to a man without his prestige, softened if it did not completely silence adverse criticism. His strict attention to detail, his perfect make-up, his energetic dash covered a multitude of faults, and he was greeted with encouraging applause as scene after scene was acted, point after point satisfactorily made, until the closing act was reached, in which his father and Booth had so often strained every power they possessed to gain the mastery. Thus far young Kean had made a most favorable impression, but the "tent scene" and Richard's desperate encounter with Richmond, have always been considered as "test *points*" upon which to base the merit of the actor, and he had wisely husbanded his energy and strength to compass the trying ordeal. He entered upon the arduous task with all the needful fire; the audience warmed to his impulsive ardor, and he had scarcely completed the exclamation "*Richard is himself again!*" when from the box adjoining the stage rang out in a clear, distinct tone, "Good boy, Charlie, worthy of your father." The outspoken enthusiast was at once recognized, and the noble criticism awarded by Junius Brutus

Booth was acknowledged by such cheers as are only vouchsafed to master spirits. Kean's grateful, heartfelt bow, as his quick eye caught a glimpse of the well known form of the *acknowledged Richard of the stage* will never be forgotten by those who were present, neither will Booth's hurried embarrassed exit when he found that he had unwittingly become the cynosure alike of audience and of stage.

Peter Ritchings is undoubtedly entitled to the next position on the roll of honor among the stock company of the Park. This is surely his due, if respectable utility is to be the decisive test. Peter was a noted and notable man on the street as well as upon the stage; for he was over six feet in stature, straight and slim as an arrow; prim and straight in all the appointments of dress, and on the promenade accompanied by his short, plump, good-natural, little wife, he was the personification of a contented presbyterian divine who considers himself in good standing with the world and his special flock. Richings was invariably well up in the varied parts of his somewhat incongruous duties on the boards, for they ranged from the mournful tragic assignment, all through the tortuous windings of the drama clear down to the funny man in farce, and farther still, he often joined in the chorus of sweet sounds when opera chanced to be the attraction; which fact may possibly account for the charming manner in which his daughter Caroline now entertains her delighted audiences. He may also in an emergency have appeared in ballet to sustain Madame Augusta in the Bayadère; if he did, it must be deemed conclusive that his long spindle-shanks did their whole duty, that the effort was a pronounced success, for Ritchings was never known to undertake any rôle and fail to create something akin to a sensation. His Dazzle, Mark Meddle, and Modus, were especially characterized by careful study and were universally admitted to be performances of unusual merit, alike by the public and the press. He was never moody or uncertain, but always appeared as one of the prominent figures of a happy family, bent on doing his utmost to promote the general weal. Ritchings was a prime favorite, not on account of sterling professional ability, but founded upon a far more enduring basis, his undeviating excellence and probity in every position of life, whether as an actor on the stage or as a man in the domestic circle.

John Fisher and his copartner John Povey divided for years the honors of low comedy. Their joint rôle included all the grave-diggers, the gawky cousins, the Yorkshire clowns, the impertinent serving-men ; in fact, everything in the pert, saucy or idiotic line fell to the lot of these comic twins. John Fisher, the brother of Mrs. Vernon, was, like that lady, of a spare and active mould, quick-witted, rare at repartee, possessed of a marvellous facial expression ; but, like the rest of his family, he was apt to chuckle perceptibly at his own comic powers. He laughed himself at his own oddities and made everyone else do the same, except his confrére Povey. This John Povey was a rotund little cockney, who looked oily from sheer good nature, but his full-moon face never betrayed the slightest emotion, yet his imperturbable gravity was irresistibly funny, and his vacant idiotic stare must have nearly equalled Liston's fit of grief, said to have convulsed his audience, for the smiles of mirth radiated through his tears; or Burton's pompous indignation, which was painfully ludicrous. The man, woman or child who could abstain from a hearty laugh when Fisher, Mrs. Vernon and Povey were on the stage was indeed a hopeless case, for no skilled medicine man could avail with such a confirmed, chronic misanthrope. Whether Povey is still alive and battling manfully with rheumatic gout, like his old friend Tom Bleakley, immured in some secluded cottage on the outskirts of civilization, condemned on dry toast and tea to do penance for the innumerable woodcock he devoured in his prime at Windust's, where ample time is given him by his former admirers for reflection and retrospection, is not known to the writer; but John Fisher died in 1847 after a brief illness, leaving Mrs. Vernon to be the last of the mirth-provoking trio.

William Wheatly was the hotspur, young villain, lover, dandy of the company. Quick, brilliant, ambitious for success in his profession, he pressed forward with determination, and at an early age became a prominent personage among a group unsurpassed for talent. His well knit, supple figure, classic features and manly bearing made him a special favorite with the ladies of the day, and the effect of their ill-concealed admiration was soon apparent in the *"petit maitre"* style, so noticeable in his subsequent walk and demeanor on the stage. But despite his vanity he rose to be recognized as a melodramatic actor of far more than ordinary merit, and ably sustained his sister, Mrs. Mason, during her short but brilliant theatrical career. On her retirement he withdrew from the Park, where he had been thoroughly and methodically schooled in stage business, and became the lessee and manager of a Philadelphia theatre, appearing only at intervals in this city, and but a short time since closed his public duties as the manager of Niblo's Garden, from which, rumor says, he retired with an ample competence.

The Mason's, Charles K. and John, came to this country with Charles Kemble and his talented daughter Fanny. As these gentlemen were nearly allied to that renowned family, they at once attracted public attention, and shone for a time from reflected splendor. While father and daughter remained on the boards the Masons were attached to their suite and enacted the *lover.* rôles when the niece of Mrs. Siddons strode the stage; for it was generally understood that the lady would not permit a stranger to breathe "soft nothings" in her ear, even in the presence of a packed audience, on a brilliantly lighted stage, and the peerless Fanny had for the moment merged her individuality into that of the impulsive Julia, and made ordinary mortals quake when in dramatic frenzy she exclaimed "Do it, nor leave the act to me." After the retirement of the Kembles, John Mason remained for a time a member of the stock company of the Park, but the lucky actor soon won the heart of a wealthy damsel of Gotham, and the twain made "assurance doubly sure" by a precipitate elopement, which created an unusual stir in methodical circles. When the parental and Knickerbocker storm had spent itself, John bade a final adieu to the stage, assiduously studied medicine, and Dr. John with Mrs. Mason soon earned professional and social distinction in the city of brotherly love, which has been for years their happy home.

Saturday night—the reverse of the present order of things, was the dull theatrical night of the week, for many occasional patrons of the drama still held to the old style idea, that all worldly matters should be cast aside at sunset of that day, and the preparations for the Sabbath formally inaugurated. Parties were inadmissible, visiting of doubtful propriety, except is cases of imperative necessity, or when the most intimate relations existed. Stars in their engagements invariably excepted Saturday nights, for these luminaries like the rest of the world had a "single eye" to the almighty dollar and had no idea of wasting their talent and time upon the unattractive walls and hard benches of the old Park. Such being the fact, it was *stock* night, but occasionally devoted to "the first appearance on any stage" of some enthusiastic worshipper of the sock and buskin school. As their debuts were as a rule not paying enterprises, the managers exacted expenses in advance from the aspirant for fame, so "par consequence" the audience of the occasion was, in classic language, *dead-head*. Debut, Saturday night, brings vividly to mind the first appearance of a stage-struck youth who had seen and studied Kemble's Romeo; had rehearsed it over and over in his leisure moments before his shaving glass, with his cot bedstead, washstand, chair and portmanteau as audience ; being his own critic, the decision was of course favorable, so he had resolved to relinquish his unromantic humdrum drudgery, become the petted hero of the horn and woo his Juliet with a pathos, in comparison with which Kemble's most tender tones would pale and be forgotten. The coming Romeo hired the Park for a Saturday night; his name was duly posted in capitals on the bills, but when the eventful time arrived, few besides the dead-heads could be induced to enter the classic portals and become "particeps criminis" in the murder of the lovesick but inoffensive Romeo. The pit, however, was comfortably filled, for the boys were always on the *qui vive* for *items*, which were not near so plentiful then as now; and besides the new star was not unknown, but chanced to be the successful and popular proprietor of the few ten pin alleys then required for the healthful well being and recreation of the young *Knicks*.

Our Romeo appeared duly togged out in full regalia, blooming as a June rose, with his courage screwed to the needful point and gained fresh confidence by the boisterous reception he met at the hands of friends in return for the free treat he was about to afford. The old actors and actresses who were to sustain the novice "had been there before" many a time, and well understood how to bolster up any faintness he might show— to aid the all-important prompter who was scarcely concealed behind the wing, and had a most arduous duty to perform. All went well at the outlet, little hitches here and there were dexterously regulated; no crash, no positive breakdown; and throughout the opening scenes the ambitious swain was sustained by visions of coming greatness, little dreaming that dread end was so close at hand; that the "balcony act" which he had rehearsed so often, and with so much confident satisfaction, in the seclusion of his quiet attic, was to prove his downfall and positively his last appearance on any stage. In this balcony act, while awaiting the appearance of his Juliet, our hero all at once seemed to realize that he was alone,—that a deathlike stillness pervaded the house; he cast wistful glances towards the supposed window, but his love was not there. In an instant all seemed chaos to the befuddled, bewildered man,—he forgot his part, was too deaf to everything to heed the almost bursting prompter. Even the audible *hems* of the convulsed Juliet were unavailing to restore consciousness,—he reeled and staggered like a drunken man, and ere assistance reached him his legs failed to perform farther duty, so our Romeo fell speechless and senseless upon the stage, amid boisterous peals of laughter from before and behind the footlights. "*Set up them pins!*" was sarcastically hurled by the critics in the pit, but all to no purpose. Fear had done its work, the green baize curtain fell— a shooting star had disappeared from the theatrical horizon—but the item-man had secured a point even on a Saturday night.

Other actors and actresses might be named and

commented on, but those already referred to may be deemed sufficient to serve as an outline of the theatrical men and women who amused and instructed us in former times at our Old Drury. The stage upon which they played, its scenery and appointments by which their efforts to please were seconded, it would be unjust to their histrionic memories to leave unnoticed; for it must recur to any one of the former habitués, who still possess the vitality and desire to visit the modern theatres, that the accessories they enjoyed were mean and pitiful when compared even with third-class establishments of to-day, and be convinced that the remembered interest they created would have been enhanced ten-fold had they been surrounded by a tithe of the gorgeous trappings and intricate machinery now deemed indispensable to success.

The stage of the Park was as spacious as was desirable for the production of any play, its dimensions having been forty by seventy feet, and Edmund Simpson was by no means a niggardly manager, for he was ever ready to avail himself of the best artistic and mechanical talent the market offered, but unfortunately for the company on the stage and the audience in front, genius in that line was a rare commodity. The public, however, were fortunately not exacting, but satisfied that the good man used his best endeavors to please; besides, in their case, for the most part, ignorance was bliss, and so perforce they were contented.

Still, as the scenery and appointments are, after the lapse of years, recalled, and in memory contrasted with the "*mise en scene*" of to-day, the whole affair seems so naked, so ridiculous, one can scarcely realize that it was tolerated for a moment, much less nightly applauded by the most cultivated people the New World could boast of. That they were cultivated and refined it is only needful to mention such names as Drake, Halleck, Bryant, Hoffman, Fay, Morris, Willis, Noah, Benjamin, Dwight, and others of the "Nobile Fratrum" whose literary labors have a world-wide repute, and who, as members of the press were rarely absent from their accustomed places in the temple of the drama.

Besides these well-known writers and poets, our merchant princes, accompanied by their families were habitual attendants, and the night was inclement when representatives of the Astors, Beekman, Hone, Coster, Douglas, Cruger, Livingston, Schermerhorn, Van Rensellaer families were not to be seen in the boxes, for such names definitely settle the quality of the auditors, who were not only satisfied with, but heartily enjoyed the primitive performance so far as stage effect was concerned.

The majority of our readers have, without doubt, visited Booth's beautiful theatre, and have witnessed with delight the magnificent artistic mountings of Hamlet at that classic establishment. Hamlet was a favorite tragedy then as it is at the present time; the critics and the public were divided then as now, with reference to the mental status of the much injured Prince of Denmark. Some actors danced about and twirled their handkerchiefs when they supposed themselves unobserved by the spies of the Queen Mother and her husband; as an evidence of joy that they had succeeded in deceiving their enemies, and beyond doubt convinced them that Hamlet was indeed what he pretended to be, stark mad; while others, who conceived themselves equally great, maintained a stoical sullenness of tone and manner throughout the five acts, which became painful from its long drawn intensity. Charles Kean was a disciple of the first class, basing his construction of the character upon the first line, "I am but mad north, northwest; when the wind is southerly I know a hawk from a handsaw," and there are some still alive who consider his rendition of the much-disputed rôle, loses nothing by comparison with greatly-admired modern delineators.

Kean's Hamlet at the Park, over thirty years ago, and Edwin Booth's personation of the same character at the present time, it is not proposed to discuss. The former was at the time pronounced unsurpassed on the stage, while the latter is the acknowledged Dane of to-day,—but it is proposed to notice the marked contrast in the stage surroundings of each; the primitive barn-like scenery and aids upon which the former was compelled to rely in his efforts for effect; and the costly elaborate appliances which must so efficiently tend to inspire and assist the latter in all the points upon which an actor relies.

Edwin Booth enacts the rôle in a princely palace, gorgeously furnished; he walks a stage on which the elaborate fitting scenery is noiselessly moved in a flash; where light and shade are so scientifically controlled and arranged, as nearly to approach the perfection of nature; nothing to mar the desired illusion, no mishap to distract either actor or spectator from the points so vital to success in the former and interest in the latter. One scene at the Old Park will suffice to demonstrate what Charles Kean was compelled to forego, so far as the actor's imagination has to do with the poet's imagery, in the supposed moonlight interview between Hamlet and the spirit of his murdered parent. The scenic artist of the Park was a man of strong, natural common sense, who, judged by his work, despised the trifling shifts of humbug; his talent developed nothing except palpable, self-evident facts. By personal observation he had ascertained that a full moon was round; he had seen one himself, and the honest man determined that the audience should have ocular demonstration of the fact without risking their health by exposure to the chilling damps.

His full moon was constructed on the most simple and economical principles. Aided by his corps of assistants, a large circular hole was cut in the center of a drop lowered at the rear of the stage, the exact altitude of which was determined by the dimensions of a step-ladder, the reach of a call-boy and the length of a tallow candle combined. This round incision was covered by a piece of the thinnest shirting muslin, so that when the long narrow box which contained the oil lamp foot-lights had been lowered out of sight, the blazing *dip* in the hand of the boy perched on the ladder, shed through the white muslin the faintest possible counterfeit glimpses of the "Queen of the Night." The daring youth in search of the parental shadow was compelled to grope his way in palpable darkness, for the stage was black as Erebus, no object discernable in the gloom save Isherwood's sickly white patch swaying backward and forward as the unsteady curtain was moved either by the wind or the restless *supe*. Eminently proper under such circumstances was it, for Hamlet to exclaim, "I'll go no farther," for it was a dangerous experiment to tread the Park stage at the imminent risk of plunging head first through one of its many traps leading to depths below.

Isherwood's lunar rays were no worse, no better than the other emanations of his artistic intellect; while the scene shifting power was limited to strong hands and willing feet, for the latter were often seen doing most diligent duty in some of the magic transformations required for the play. With such surroundings it will readily be perceived that Kean had few extraneous props upon which to lean, but was compelled to achieve deserved reputation by his individual powers.

Now and then by chance, a few of the Old Park fogies do meet and chat about theatricals as they were, and as they are. On the question of mechanical skill and artful, sensational display, they with one accord cry beaten. They concede the dramatic temples of Young America to be magnificent, and relate with *bated breath*, the new marvels they beheld in the modern homes of the Muses; they slyly tell of peeps at the enchanting Forty Thieves, of the enticements of the Twelve

Temptations, or go into ecstacies about the witcheries of Opera Bouffé, and chuckle over the lavish exhibition of charms; grow practical when the Ballet is mentioned, but are vacillating and unsatisfactory on the all-absorbing controversy of blonde *versus* brunette—they as one man concur in the wish that they were boys again, for in their hearts they mourn over the unromantic times in which their youth was a part, for then all these delightful things were not. But when the key note of pure legitimate is sounded, they warm up and are anxious to compare one by one the old time favorites with the new lights, stripped of all modern improvements; and they boldly assert that in this respect tinsel and show have usurped the place of pure gold on the American stage.

The Park had its day, but during the last few years of its existence it was shorn of much of its former prestige. The National Theatre was new, its managers young and energetic, all its appointments in keeping with the advance of the city. Under the management of Thos. S. Hamblin the doors of the Park were kept open, but the venerable pile was burned to the ground in 1845, during an engagement of the Montplaisir troup of dancers, when its name and fame became the property of the dusty past.

The building now standing and known as the Bowery Theatre is the third dramatic temple which has been erected on the same ground. Its predecessors were destroyed by fire, the present structure having been raised in 1836. The prominent managers in its glorious days were

Dinneford, who was succeeded by Thomas S. Hamblin. Both were peculiar favorites with the singular and clannish patrons of that section of the city.

It was at the Bowery the first scintillations of Edwin Forrest's stentorian powers were brought prominently into notice. Leggatt, the editor of the *Evening Post*, was the champion of this American tragedian, and availed himself of every opportunity to laud the performances of his special pet. Forrest's marvellous physique was the pride and delight of the Bowery boys, who have always been noted for their admiration of the intensely sensational order. The "blood and thunder" school of declamation was to them "a joy forever," and young Forrest seemed fitted by nature to fill their exalted idea of grandeur. His original Metamora and Jack Cade, or his Spartacus was sure to fill the house with an enthusiastic crowd.

Tom Hamblin, the manager, was also a sure card with the east-side patrons. His commanding figure, expansive chest, jet flowing locks, and *stagey* strut, realized their conception of Adonis. He was well posted in all the tricks of the trade, and until his voice was seriously injured by an asthmatic complaint, he could bellow with the best, "tear a passion to tatters, to very rags," "split the ears of the groundlings," and thus made himself a hero with men and boys who doted on caricature, no matter what shape it assumed, always provided there was a strong infusion of the grandiloquent.

John R. Scott was far from being an insignificant imitator of Forrest, and undoubtedly ranked next on the list of Bowery stars. Like his adored pattern his style was that of the expansive school, and in classic vernacular, " he spread himself,"— "No pent up Utica confined his powers," as the capacious stage of the Bowery was none too large for the complete exhibition of his melo-dramatic frenzy, when in the closing scene he was surrounded by blue flames, and wildly hi-hied by the thoroughly roused *B'hoys* who were packed in the pit at a shilling a head.

This Bowery pit was doubtless the study from which emanated the current theological idea that the theatre was the visible "counterfeit presentment" of that mythological terror so persistently dwelt on by the good dominies to deter the Knickerbocker youth from entering its doors. The patrons of this pit were little devils of every shape and shade, with a large preponderance of the printer's imp, backed up by his sworn ally in wickedness, the newspaper boy; who was and still remains a zealous supporter of the drama, and has an abiding faith in stunning effects on the stage. There free, outspoken critics were nightly at their posts, and when the doors were opened rushed like unchained demons to secure front seats. Woe betide the luckless stranger who in the furious mêlée had chanced to light upon the chosen spot of some steady attendant, for with the cry of "hustle him out," the intruder was passed to the rear as if he were nothing but an inanimate mass, from bench to bench, by the hatless, coatless, barefooted crew, with a practiced dexterity which baffles description. This unwashed, uncombed assemblage were unmistakable believers in the doctrines set forth by the great English traveler, so far as the conduct of the occupants of the first tier was concerned; for even the careless turning of the back upon their domain was quickly detected, and as quickly righted by the well-understood shout of *Trollope;* and when the imperative order had been complied with, the impolite offender was comforted by a rousing cheer. At the tinkle of the bell, "down in front," "hats off," announced from the pit that the thrilling scenes were to be enacted, and for a time the pandemonium was silent as the grave.

Josephine Clifton was for a time the ruling theatrical goddess of the Bowery. She seemed, as it were, expressly created to meet the extravagant ideas of her worshippers, so far as dimensions went. Though of gigantic proportions for a woman, her form was symmetrical, her features attractive and her voice not lacking in sweetness of tone. Macbeth, even personated by the stalwart Forrest, or the long-striding Hamblin, looked insignificant and puny when the magnificent towering Joe Clifton walked the stage as their "better-half," while the other actors and actresses dwindled into mere pigmies by her side. This theatrical giantress was, however, short lived, and her sister, Miss Missouri, who was almost her counterpart in physical development and personal charms ended her brief career on the stage, as was currently reported at the time, by poison. But by far the best actress which the Bowery could boast of in the olden times was Mrs. Shaw, afterwards the wife of Manager Hamblin. For years this lady sustained the leading female rôles with marked ability, and some of her impersonations would compare favorably with the best then known on the English or American stage. Mrs. Shaw was an admirable reader; but little inclined to rant, and apparently gave no heed to the claptrap nonsense so generally in vogue with those whose lot was cast to please critics with a taste so decided as that which swayed the verdicts of the Bowery pit. The purely sensational even constrained the great Booth, when in his latter days he now and then gratified the *boys* with his far-famed *Richard*, and the old stager knew full well that it was needful to husband his strength for the closing act. He knew that a short, decisive conflict with Richmond would not do; that nothing but a long-drawn, "rough and tumble," exhausting fight would come up to the standard. Flynn and other aspiring Richmonds were on more than one occasion the victims of Booth's energetic display; for the cheers of the *unterrified* seemed to rekindle the latent fires of the veteran, who dealt blows right and left, which were not laid down in the rehearsed programme; and with a will which often caused his opponent to dance about with a dexterity seldom witnessed on the boards, and these Richmonds always seemed to feel a great sense of relief, when the doughty crooked-back tyrant relaxed his spasmodic efforts and permitted himself to be dispatched, as laid down in Shakespeare's version of the tragedy.

CHAPTER FOURTEENTH.

The Franklin Theatre, situated on Chatham Square was a cheap, small concern and a weak competitor of the Bowery. Its rivalry amounted to little notwithstanding the fact that Booth was occasionally entrapped in his eccentric wanderings and induced to appear for one or two nights. There were, however, two sensations at this house which attracted notice and brought many dollars into the treasury. The hero of the first was a stage-struck genius named Kirby who drew crowds to witness his death-throes in the closing scene of Richard. In intensity and protracted horror they surpassed anything ever attempted up to that period, for by comparison Booth's highest pressure under the direct influence of both outward and inward spirit was tame and insipid. Kirby, in imitation of the Junius Brutus, kept his vitality well in hand for the final *wind up*, and his audience, as if in sympathy, listlessly reclined until the moment came, when the hitherto harmless and apparently peaceful man was to commence his "high and lofty tumbling" as if he had just been stung by a thousand wasps. "Wake me up when Kirby dies" was a cant saying of the time, but the man or boy who could sleep during Kirby's agonizing howlings, could calmly repose in the embrace of a yelping maniac.

The other feature which recurs in connection with the this theatre was the production of the local drama in which Mose, Sikesy and Lize are introduced as types of the peculiar class then known as Bowery B'hoys, or Fire-laddies. The allusions and situations, combined with the peculiar phraseology of the leading characters, invested the piece with unusual interest, and insured it a temporary popularity. Male citizens of every grade, after investing in a pint of freshly-roasted peanuts, betook themselves to witness Chanfrau's admirable personation of the reckless, devil-may-care, yet chivalric Mose, whose oddities have been already noticed in a preceding chapter, where the reader has met him in *propria persona*, and can perhaps comprehend the difficulties which beset even that talented actor in his endeavors to faithfully portray a character which has now become obsolete and a legend of the past.

The opening of the National Theatre, on the northwest corner of Church and Leonard streets, marked a new era in our theatricals. The auditorium was constructed with some regard to comfort, and by comparison with the old places of amusement in Gotham it appeared grand and luxurious. It was originally designed to be the home of Italian Opera in the new world, but after a short season of financial disaster, the unacclimated singing birds became disgusted with the chilling associations of the temperate zone, and took wing for more sunny climes. Our venerable friend, John Falstaf Hackett, took possession of the abandoned nest ere it became cold, and dedicated it to dramatic entertainments of the Anglo-Saxon type. For a time, under the management of this well-known "Sergeant of the Old Guard," it thrived apace, but its renown was assured when James W. Wallack came to the rescue and assumed entire control. His enterprise, tact and histrionic ability were untiringly devoted to its success, and it was at the National that he laid the foundation for his long and brilliant career as a metropolitan manager of rare accomplishments.

The stock company was culled with great discrimination from the theatrical ranks at home as well as from abroad; and the comedy staff was most admirably chosen, for such names recur as Mitchell, "Billy Villiams of the Vells," Browne, Blake, Nickerson, who were in themselves a host never to be forgotten, while the memory of a hearty laugh remains to warm up the stagnant blood. Browne's "Robert Macaire," and the "Jacques Strop" of Williams, were gems of comic acting that the intervention of long years cannot dim—they can scarcely blur the much-enjoyed treat.

During Wallack's management he made a most marked hit by the introduction of English opera. The troupe was a choice one, and it had a long and successful engagement. The favorite singers were Mesdames Sheriff, Seguin and Poole, who were most ably supported by Messrs. Wilson and Seguin. Balfe's "Amilie" was brought out, and it miraculously *fitted* the Yankee idea of music, which was, and is, no matter what may be assured to the contrary, ringing, cheerful, simple melody, for "Morning's Ruddy Beams Tinged the Eastern Sky" and "My Boyhood's Home" were for the time warbled in the parlors and carolled on the streets of Gotham. Wallack did not then, as was his custom of late years, rely entirely upon the attractions of his unsurpassed stock company. The stars of the period were frequently engaged, and among them were the Vanderhoffs, father, son and daughter. The elder Vanderhoff was a most finished elocutionist; his readings in Cato were superb, while his personation of Cardinal Richelieu, penned expressly to display the peculiar powers of the much-eulogized Macready, has not been surpassed by a single one of the many who have attempted its delineation on the American stage. The daughter was a polished, finished actress, and her "Pauline," a test character of the day, ranked with the best, while the son, who has made his home with us for many a year, is too well known, far and wide, on the stage and in the lecture room, to need the tribute even of a passing notice.

When theatrical planets were not available, Rolla, Don Cæsar, Evelin, or any one of *The Wallack's* artistic rôles was sure to fill the house, for from his first entrée at the Park he was stamped as guinea gold by public opinion, and to the end held his high rank. All agreed that he was a most finished actor, and possessed the happy faculty of being invariably agreeable to his audience. Though he did not entirely sink his individuality, he deserves great credit for his marked endeavor to cloak the *Wallackian* vanity, for which that family is so noted, both on and off the stage. James W. Wallack, as an actor, displayed so much ability that his vanity was most cheerfully pardoned by his enthusiastic admirers.

On his second visit to this country, Charles Kean appeared at the National; but ere his engagement closed, and when the stage was set for Richard, the popular theatre was burned and never rebuilt. Wallack's subsequent theatrical life belongs to the modern era.

When the National Theatre was destroyed, the sons and daughters of Melpomene who had domiciled there, were scattered hither and thither. Mitchell, an unmistakable child of Momus, established himself as the manager of a tiny box situated on Broadway, between Howard and Grand streets, which he dignified with the name of theatre and christened the laugh-provoking nook as "The Olympic." This seven by nine cubby-hole he devoted to sensational burlesque, and the manager in person was its bright particular star throughout its prosperous career. His corps of assistants was of course very limited in number, for the stage was scarcely more spacious than an ordinary parlor, but as regarded fitness for the business required it was a rare combination. Mitchell, Walcott, Nickerson, Clarke, Mary Taylor, Misses Nickerson and Clarke were the fixed attractions, though others were in an emergency temporarily engaged, among whom was Stephen Massett, who of late has become widely known as the famous "Jeemes Pipes, of Pipeville," a wandering philosopher, who, "when the moon o'er the lake is beaming" hies away to the uttermost p——— of the cars, to cull fresh stimulants for his restless muse. Massett made his début in the operatic line, and ably assisted in the travesties of Fra Diavolo and Amelia. Mitchell, however, was his own best card; he was a wonderful mimic. Nast, with his pencil is great; Mitchell, with nothing but his stubby frame was far greater, and no actor or actress of note escaped his trenchant, ironical burlesque.

His caricatures of Booth's Richard, Kean's Hamlet and Forrest's Othello were marvels of grotesque imitation, but his crowning success was as a "Danseuse," at the time when the *divine* Fanny Elsler was creating sad havoc among New Yorkers, old and young; causing her slaves to cut up all sorts of anti-Knickerbocker antics, for a most prominent one was carried so far by his infatuation that the *Poetess of Motion* was whirled up the Bloomingdale road behind his showy four-in-hand, to the unspeakable horror of grandfathers and the ill-concealed envy of the boys who were not so fortunate as to represent the capitalists of the *Mam*.

Elsler had selected for her "pièce de resistance" at the Park a ballet entitled La Tarantule, and on each appearance the queen of agile grace was literally showered with bouquets, which were hurled at her with the wildest enthusiasm. Mitchell, with his quick sense of the ludicrous, fully appreciated the demented condition of affairs, and his cogitations culminated in the production of a ballet at the Olympic, with himself as the rival of the then inimitable posturist and dancer.

On the first night of "The Mosquitoe" there was scarcely breathing room in his little theatre for an hour before the curtain was to rise, for expectation was on tip-toe, curiosity was rife as to what extent this new tried imitation would be a success.

Mitchell's costume and make-up were exact copies of the original, but any attempt to describe the effect they produced when fitted upon his well-known figure, is utterly vain. Imagine a short, thick-set man, with heavy, bandy legs, and red, full moon, comical face, arrayed in short lace petticoats, his dumpty extremities encased in flesh-colored tights, white satin slippers on his goodly-sized feet, streamers of gay ribbons fluttering from his broad shoulders, his big round head encircled by a wreath of bright flowers, standing before you in a position of exaggerated grace, and with a fearful assumption of modesty, tremulously bowing to a perfect storm of cheers, and some faint conception may be formed of the nondescript apparition advertised to personate the most accomplished dancing woman of the age.

In the item of graceful repose, Ellsler by common consent won the day; but when the item of agility comes to be discussed, critics were divided, for Mitchell performed wonders in the jumping line that were instigated by his arduous efforts to prevent his airy apparel from unduly rising and thus possibly shock the more sensitive of his refined audience. The closing scene of La Tarantule as performed by Ellsler was pronounced the "acme" of graceful power, for Fanny's aerial flights were stupenduous; they carried Young

America to the very verge of hopeless lunacy. Mitchell's genius was, however, equal to such an emergency. He brought rope and hook into requisition to aid him in his determined resolve not to be outdone by a woman, and the burly humorist was through their agency hoisted high in air, where he kicked and floundered until the spectators were worn out with laughter, when he displayed a placard which triumphantly informed the public "*that he could jump higher and stay longer than Fanny ever could.*"

On being lowered from his giddy height Mitchell "pirouetted" for a while, embowered in carrots, turnips, parsnips and onions, and when backing out gave vent to his overflowing feelings with the simple broken words "*Tousan tank, me art too fool*," and which the arch knave had stolen bodily from the idol of the hour. Ellsler on more than one occasion witnessed the side-splitting contortions of Mitchell, and rewarded the incomparable mimic with genuine marks of her appreciation.

Mitchell, with all his smooth sailing, had some trouble now and then to manage the characters who made the Olympic pit their rendezvous. Among them there was a sprinkling of news-boys, who, from being mere peddlers of papers, had through continuous contact with these *mediums of lore* become educated and graduated into noisy critics, who never hesitated to express their likes and dislikes in the most positive, even boisterous manner. With this pit Mary Taylor was a deity. "Our Mary" was an all-important personage, and whoever ventured to speak slightingly of their adopted queen was quieted in the most summary manner. It so chanced that on one occasion "Our Mary" and the worthy manager came to a misunderstanding relative to some matter behind the scenes—a mere matter of increase of salary. Mitchell refused to comply; "Our Mary" refused to go on; so when the curtain rose, Miss Clarke, a gentle, modest girl, appeared in the place that "Our Mary" had heretofore filled to the unspeakable satisfaction of her rough admirers. The Olympic pitites took in the situation at a glance, and with one accord demanded the restitution of their pet. They hooted at the inoffensive substitute, bellowed "fresh shad" in the shrillest possible key, varying only the monotony by occasional yells for Mary and Mitchell to appear. After a few moments "Old Crummles," calm as a spring morn, walked to the footlights amid cheers mingled with the shout "Put Mary back!" "Where is our Mary?" When comparative silence was obtained, Mitchell's face and manner were a study not often seen, as he looked upon the riotous crew and slowly uttered: "I attend to my own business in my own way. If there is any more disturbance in the pit I shall raise the price!" The manager retired with applause; the play of the "Savage and the Maiden" proceeded without further interruption, Mary Taylor was restored, and she continued to delight her enthusiastic knights until her marriage, when she bade adieu to the stage.

A play was run for a short period at the Olympic which was a source of much merriment to the initiated, but was the cause of many embarrassing incidents to those who chanced to be novices and ignorant of its intent. While the piece was progressing on the stage, several of the actors were disguised, and mingled with the audience to enact their *roles* at the proper time. On a certain occasion a well known and conspicuous resident of Gotham was seated in the boxes, and intent upon the play which he had never seen or heard of. Next him sat a person in rustic attire, a well-to-do countryman in appearance and manners, whose whole attention seemed also to be riveted upon the play. Suddenly the hitherto quiet farmer sprang to his feet, and in tones of the most intense excitement implored his long lost wife to quit that stage and return to her abandoned home, and at the same time appealed to the gentleman who sat bewildered beside him to aid him in the recovery of his stolen treasure, who was fully aware from the shouts of "Shame! shame! put him out!" that the eyes of the audience were fixed upon him, and he keenly felt his perplexed and ridiculous position. The more he smoothed his irate neighbor, whispering that he knew Mitchell well; that he would use every effort to restore the fallen angel to her lord, the more boisterous became the excited husband, and the louder seemed the surrounding uproar. It was not until the curtain was lowered that he discovered the inconsolable man had flown. The storm of the audience was changed to peals of hearty laughter, when the kind sympathetic gentleman perceiving at a glance the presence of the "little joker," modestly retired, and ever after took high ground against practical jokes in any form. For genuine fun New York has had no successor to the Olympic. Mitchell was a preacher indeed when he took upon him the task of ridiculing the follies and extravagancies of the times.

The inception of Niblo's Suburban Pleasure Ground, which is now covered by the Metropolitan Hotel, a magnificent theatre and a concert hall, was an advance step taken by William Niblo, who had acquired a down-town reputation as a caterer, and in consequence became famous among the *bon vivants* and the critical tasters of fruity *lachrymæ*. This new summer retreat was remote from the dust and bustle of the city proper, quite a little walk from the densely populated quarters, and its simple arrangements and ornamentation were deemed fully up to the mark of the modest ruling taste. A plain board fence enclosed most of the property on the block bounded by Prince, Houston, Broadway and Crosby Street, and on the south-east corner on Broadway was built the bar-room, saloon, or whatever name would now be given to the apartment devoted to spirituous refreshment; it was both spacious and airy, and it at once became the chosen rendezvous of a set of men well known in the city, who spent their money freely at convivial meetings. These worthy citizens were past middle age and disposed to be very glum and ill-natured if their classic seances were disturbed or interrupted by Young America, either during their afternoon entertainment at Cato's or their soiree at Niblo's; so the young.

sters were apt to give the latter place a wide berth, and left the distinguished guardians of Cape Fear, Cape Lookout, and other prominent corners of the promenade in undisputed possession of the field, where under the leadership of the renowned Cedar Street ship merchants, the worthy fathers spun their yarns into the "wee sma' hours," washing them down with frequent copious libations, in memoriam of their struggles in the battle of life. This set of ancient revellers gave to Niblo's bar-room a widespread notoriety, and it soon became a source of considerable income to its accommodating, genial proprietor.

To the garden proper there was a separate entrance from Broadway for the accommodation of such visitors whose tastes inclined them to seek umbrageous bowers for the full enjoyment of ice cream, cooling port wine negus or refreshing lemonade. This department was under the immediate supervision of Mrs. Niblo, who, whatever may be averred to the contrary, was the ruling spirit of this enterprise, for she secured the "income" and watched the "out-go" with such rare business ability that the place acquired a name and fame enduring still, not blotted out by the march of modern improvement.

The walks were trimly kept, the beds filled with a choice variety of shrubs and flowers; cages with singing birds were suspended here and there among the branches; settees with little tables were ranged beneath the trees or placed in tasteful vine-clad summer houses, and in the evening this New York paradise was illuminated by the agency of numberless lanterns of particolored glass of the glow-worm type, whose effulgence possessed the merit of not being trying to the complexion and did away with the necessity of lily white and rouge, so essential to effect in the strong glare of blazing gaslight. Everything about the Garden evidenced careful supervision: order and neatness lent a charm to the inexpensive appointments.

In the centre of the plot Niblo caused to be erected an open saloon, which was devoted to such light entertainment as is afforded by instrumental and vocal music, vaudeville or "piquante" farce, with rollicking John Sefton in the cast. As after a brief space it became eminently proper for the fair sex, under the protection of a well assured escort, to visit Niblo's Saloon, the proprietor was compelled to enlarge his accommodations in the dramatic line. By degrees the Saloon grew to the proportions of a real theatre, and the latter swept away garden, walk, shrub, tree and bower, and though the name of Garden was retained, scarcely a vestige of a green plant was left as a witness of the original plan. Even Mrs. Niblo removed her headquarters, and nightly supervised the unromantic details of the ticket office, that she might, with more certainty, gather the increasing influx of dollars, and by her presence dam the many infinitesmal outlets through which shillings and sixpences are said to unaccountably flow and be forever lost to the trusting manager.

The great Ravel family of gymnasts, dancers and contortionists was the first grand card Niblo secured, with the lithe, graceful Gabriel as leader in their marvellous feats of pantomime, and for many consecutive seasons crowded houses greeted their nightly re-entrée. As time rolled on the beautiful dramatic temple on the rear of the old garden was built, when Billy Niblo, abundantly blessed with stacks of dollars, in modern estimation, " Heaven's best gift to man," retired to enjoy the fruits of his long services to a generous and appreciative public.

The Lafayette and Richmond Hill Theatres were incipient abortions, and would not be considered worthy of remembrance were it not that by chance each was associated with the recollection of marked men who have figured in the city. The first named was located on Laurens Street, just north of Canal, which, at the period (1828), must have been a most unpromising tract; for the neighborhood was sparsely settled, and the few inhabitants little likely to be tempted by the allurements of the stage. During its brief existance, however, this temple of the muses was under the management of no less a man than Charles W. Sandford, for years one of the legal lights of the New York bar, but far more widely known as the Major General commanding the forces designated as the First Division, New York State Militia. The presumption is, the young advocate and embryo military leader was considerably out of pocket by this speculation, for soon after it was opened to the public the house was burned, and was never rebuilt.

The Richmond Hill, another short-lived, feeble attempt to establish a place of amusement remote from the traveled highways, was on Charlton street near Varick, then one of the most quiet sections of the city, in fact beyond its actual limit. Its high-sounding name was derived from the site it occupied, and a portion of the altered building had formerly been the country residence of Aaron Burr, when that schemer was at the full of his political career, and who in his pride had so christened the slight elevation upon which it rested. From the start it proved a wretched undertaking; even the few dead-head "claquers" of the time objected to travel so far from their accustomed rounds, and as its associations were not worthy of notice by the respectable press, the date is not published when its green baize curtain was finally lowered.

One other dingy mongrel place, where people were wont to congregate, is brought to mind by the recollection of "anniversary week;" a week unmistakably designated by the influx of a horde of cadaverous-looking outsiders that came "cawing" into town from far and from near, togged out in shiny black swallow-tails, and uniformed with blue cotton umbrellas, white cravats, black cotton gloves, and each pilgrim armed with a long, lank carpet bag, in which to transport all its owner could not possibly devour during the crusade. These hungry-looking worshippers of "isms" gave the hotels a wide berth; they came to gorge not disgorge, they quartered upon the faithful of the city without even deigning to go through the formality of a simple "by your leave." During the six days of their pilgrimage at the shrine of Fanaticism the altar was erected at the

Broadway Tabernacle, and the place rang with discordant yells at all hours, day and night, when the locusts were not employed in satisfying their inward cravings.

This tabernacle was an unsightly pile which for many years disfigured Broadway, but it was a hall of considerable capacity, and its acoustic qualities said to be the very best in the city. It was originally designed for a free Congregational church, but for some time before its demolition either it or its proprietors fell from grace and it became common stamping ground, on which all classes and conditions of men and women ventilated their religious fanatical or political reveries. Wendell Phillips, W. Lloyd Garrison, Gerrett Smith, Arthur Tappan, Lucretia Mott and kindred spirits of the unadulterated abolition stripe, made the old walls ring again with their soul-stirring recitals of the wrongs to suffering Sambo, in the incipient stage of the emancipation crusade.

Owing, however, to its accessibility it was frequently hired for concerts and musical entertainments by artists of great merit. Ole Bull and Vieuxtemps enlivened it with the "Carnival of Venice." Braham and DeBegnies made it ring again with their powerful voices; Charles E. Horn and Austin Phillips often carrolled there their sweetest notes, and even the mighty Barnum for a time entertained the idea of introducing his Swedish nightingale at the Tabernacle; but the shrewd calculator discovered at the last moment that far off Castle Garden, away down by the sounding sea, would hold one more on a pinch and thus warrant the sale of still another ticket at the famous auction. This auction plan was adopted by the great and good temperance orator as the only method by which he could satisfy the public and at the same time save himself from the imputation of favoritism during the furore excited by the appearance of Jenny Lind. That auction was a great success; the price paid by the hatter for his ticket, was a marvellous dodge in the advertising line; it was the highest flight of circus imagery. The Mermaid, Joyce Heth, the Wooly Horse, Tom Thumb, all paled before it. The Duke of Iranistan was by it raised to a bewildering elevation in the esteem of an appreciative constituency.

CHAPTER FIFTEENTH.

Three or four decades since, society did not as a rule keep its carriage, fashion did not exact it, neither was the then moderate expense necessary to respectability; so that one of the most notable changes which has taken place is in the number and luxurious costliness of the vehicles which now meet the eye. It is only a few years since that all the private carriages seen on Broadway or the Bloomingdale Road were as well known to any observant citizens as were the faces and names of the owners. The half-dozen negro coachmen in livery were marked objects for comment, and the solitary footman clad in green and gold lace, in the employ of a lady long noted for her eccentric display, sat in a dejected mood on the "dickey," as if ashamed of his toggery and menial vocation. There were two four-in-hand teams, one driven by Mr. John Hunter, of Hunter's Island, near New Rochelle, a gentleman of leisure and large wealth; the other, the property of Henry Marx, the noted exquisite of his day, who possessed sufficient independence of spirit to take one step ahead, to bid defiance to the sombre habiliments of the time, and who was almost tabooed for his marked departure from established custom—the dashing, genial Harry Marx, who for many years had the exclusive title of "Dandy" prefixed to his name. But the spirit and unequalled style of his four "high-bred" chestnuts enabled him to bear with perfect nonchalance the sneers and jealousies that beset him on every side, and while he lived and flourished no man in Gotham enjoyed life with a finer zest than Dandy Marx. The ponderous Tilbury of a well-known importer who hailed from the Green Isle, and whose descendants are now prominent in society, was a great feature on the drive, his powerful seventeen-hand bay, glossy, proud, and as quick-stepping as a pony, was universally admired when driven to the unwieldy two-wheeled drag. Many will recall the high-perched seat of the dashing, briefless, but wealthy young lawyer who lived "away up town," at the Carlton House, on the corner of Broadway and Leonard street; the open barouche of the gay Cedar street silk merchant to be seen any fine afternoon, except Sunday, occupied by a select stag party en route for Burnham's and Cato's; the yellow coach with heavy *hammer cloth,* in waiting for its lady owner who resided on the corner of Broadway and Tin-Pot Alley; the low, comfortable carriage, slowly drawn for years by a pair of fat, lazy, long-tailed bays, trained in the good old days when there was little to do and plenty of time in which to perform that little. This latter establishment formed a complete combination; the owner determined upon ease after a life of slow but sure usefulness; the staid old driver whose head seemed to nod in perfect accord with the measured tread of the well-fed quadrupeds; the low, swinging, roomy vehicle, wherein reclined a retired Scotch merchant, the picture of calm content and good will toward all mankind, a spirit which has descended to an only son, who still lives to bestow liberal yet unostentatious gifts to the friendless and stricken, from the abundant estate bequeathed to his stewardship. The well-known gig of the world-renowned surgeon, whose neat Quaker garb, highly-polished white top boots, low-crowned, broad-brimmed, well-brushed beaver were as familiar to all classes as the commonest necessity of daily life; for all, rich and poor, young and old, felt respect and love for Valentine Mott. The neat equipage of the tall, courtly Mayor, Philip Hone, standing in front of his residence on Broadway, opposite the Park, which in 1835 was swept away with others belonging to the Astors to give place to the then grand Astor House.

A few more private carriages might be specified, all as familiarly known to every urchin as was the most direct route to Stuart's candy store, located on the corner of Greenwich and Chambers streets, a pound of whose "broken mixed candy" was considered the acme of juvenile bliss.

A carriage was not a necessity. The limits of the city proper were so circumscribed that ladies could visit and shop without fatigue, and the man who ventured to drive to his store, counting-room or office, would have been pronounced a parvenu with scarcely a dissenting voice. There were *Hackney Coaches*; rickety, dilapidated concerns, whose very appearance indicated that they were employed only in cases of dire necessity. Fortunately, if only on the score of decency, these creaking vehicles were not an essential part of a funeral, as it was the decorous custom for mourners and their friends to walk to the grave in solemn procession, headed by the dominie robed in full canonicals.

Horses kept merely for pleasure, owned in the city, and driven to light wagons (?)—an etherial Ford or Godwin, celebrated makers, would weigh three hundred pounds at least—were seldom seen on the lower portion of Broadway; the rough cobble-stone pavement was not benficial to light springs; but the more important objection lay in the fact that when a young man was seen during business hours, certain prominent citizens would place a black mark against his social credit, and sundry venerable dames would audibly predict that the money which had been so carefully accumulated by the departed parent, would soon be squandered by reckless waste. These steady old gentlemen and precious old ladies rarely put in an appearance on the then famous Third Avenue and Cato Lane, and therefore knew nothing of the pranks of *Young America* and his 2.40 trotter as he whizzed past Hazard's and the Red House, self-satisfied and proud as though he were pulling the reins over Dexter or Pocahontas on Harlem Lane and dusting the youthful commodore. There are doubtless some readers who can recall the time when Harlem, the present Twelfth Ward, now being so rapidly covered with dwellings and costly mansions was but an expanse of fields and sold as farming land by the acre. What is now Madison Square, surrounded by insurmountable brick walls which were the terror of the comparatively few juvenile offenders against the laws of the city. At this point cobble stones stopped and the road, or drive in modern parlance, began. Land speculators of the day looked upon the rural suburb lying beyond as "a far off country," too remote even to be available as city lots. The financial crash of 1837 darkened the hopes of many an aspiring genius; while the old fogy spirit, more rife then than now, opposed everything that bore the semblance of progress.

At this period there were but few noticeable residences north of the city limits. Here and there a country seat on the Hudson or East River, the home of some sly Knickerbocker who buried a few dollars in a few acres of rocky land, whose descendants now roll in untold wealth from the timely venture of their far-seeing ancestors.

Conspicuous among these domains was the mansion of Charles Henry Hall. His prominent estate was located at the upper end of the easterly side of the Island, and its northern boundary was washed by the Harlem River, then the resort of amateur fishermen, as it was celebrated for bass and its waters were undisturbed by steamboats and untainted by the refuse of factory or sewer. The natural beauties which distinguished the home of Mr. Hall were cultivated with a lavish hand; broad avenues lined with forest trees led to well arranged flower gardens, ornamented with artificial ponds and other tasty appliances which rendered the place one of the main attractions to visitors from abroad. Mr. Hall was one of the few northern gentlemen who was devotedly interested in the noble horse; his stalls were filled with noted racers of the purest strain, and as a sequence he was courted by the prominent spirits of the turf, who shared with the generous proprietor his love for field sports unmixed with the *Hippodrome* trickery and modern swindling practices which, of late years, have brought disgrace upon the race-course both in this country and in England. Could Charles Henry Hall, Col. Johnston of Virginia, Gibbons of New Jersey, W. J. Porter of the *Spirit of the Times*, with scores of other lovers of the horse who might be named, "revisit the pale glimpses of the moon," they would hail with delight the advent of Jerome Park, and bid the American Jockey Club godspeed in their endeavor to return the lost prestige of racing and redeem the turf from the filth which late years have strewn around that once dignified and manly sport.

The old Hall mansion still stands, shorn of its broad acres and commanding attractions. Modern improvement is fast sweeping away the landmarks of the past generation and will soon decree its utter annihilation, when it will be remembered only for a short time by the few survivors who in years gone by partook of the princely hospitality dispensed within its walls while listening to the learned disquisitions of the assembled guests on the rival strains of blooded stock for the turf or road.

In those days Third Avenue was the trotting road over which our sires exercised their favorite nags. Hostelries dotted the drive at convenient distances, at which man and beast could procure the needed refreshment, and they were furnished as now with broad piazzas from which horsemen could scan and discuss the merits of the flyers.

They had trotters in those days, and good ones, too,—Dexter, Lady Thorn, Goldsmith Maid, American Girl, Mountain Boy, Butler, and a few more noted ones may have knocked some seconds from the 2:40 standard of speed, but Dutchman, Confidence, Abdallah, Rifle, Ned Forrest, Peggy Magee, Ice Pony, etc., yet hold a good position on the records of fast time, while Dutchman's three mile time is unexpunged, and still challenges the efforts of Young America.

In our mind's eye we can see those quadrupeds of the past champing the bit under Cato's shed, then one of the noted halting places of the road. This Cato was a famous man in his generation. A sable son of Africa he lived and died respected in a community far more aristocratic and exclusive than its more pretentious democratic successors, yet it was unbiased by any tinge of modern abolition doctrine, a community which knew nothing of sensational *issues*. Cato was black, but long intimate contact with the gentlemen he served had imparted to his gentle, modest nature an unpretending dignity of manner, which won the esteem of all who approached him and secured for his humble house of entertainment such a wide-spread reputation, that for years it was one of the prominent resorts of our citizens and attracted many of the prominent sight-seers who made pilgrimages to the Island of Manhattan.

Cato's house was located on a side road, or lane, as it was called, leading from the Third Avenue nearly opposite the point where the old shot-tower still stands, and in close proximity to the summer residence of the Beekman family, then as now large landed proprietors. The quaint old bar-room and diminutive sitting-room with their sanded floors were scrupulously neat, the coarse whitewashed walls covered with odd engravings of the olden time, would prove rare curiosities to-day; but they, with their proprietor, have long since passed away. Piles of brick and mortar now occupy the site where Cato daily dispensed creature comforts to the Hones, Carters, Beekmans, Tallmadges, Janeways, Van Cortlandts, etc., with their many friends.

After buying our cigars—*cigars;*—the name recalls the fact that Cato sold five cigars for one shilling,—real cigars at that; no Dutch cabbage leaves with Connecticut wrappers, for when enjoyed they emitted an aroma which would shame articles now disposed of at twenty-five cents each by our leading Broadway shops. The reader will please bear in mind that a *dollar* had some weight in those primitive days, and that it was treated with some considerable respect by the fortunate possessor, for it would buy three times the amount of food or pleasure that can now be procured with its modern representative. Dollars, like our population, have increased in numbers; quantity not quality is now the rage, and the man who thirty years since had an income of five thousand dollars, could enjoy all the comforts now within the reach of the possessor of twenty. At that time many of the extravagant luxuries of to-day were unknown, but a glass of Cato's brandy (price six and a quarter cents) cannot now be obtained on the road at any figure. Bourbon whisky perhaps has a tendency to develop more speed, as a little of that delectable beverage "goes a great way." So let's drop that question and swing up the Lane.

Cato's Lane, long since closed, was one of the *spurting* spots on the drive. It was a semi-circular road about three-quarters of a mile in length, leading from the Third Avenue and again meeting it at a point not far distant from the spot on which now stands the Third Avenue Railroad Depot at Sixty-Fifth Street. No steel rail was then dreamt of on the avenue, neither was any needed for the traffic. The few scattered dwellers of Yorkville and Harlem were amply accommodated by a line of stages, which passed at intervals of two or three hours, and in due course of time, for there was no hurry then, landed their human freight at Park Row or Harlem Bridge as the case might be; where, after the driver had refreshed his inner man, and to the best of his ability divided the receipts of the trip between himself and the proprietors, leisurely started on the return journey. The appointments of this stage enterprise can be vividly recalled if one chances to meet one of the present High Bridge lines struggling up Manhattanville Hill. Omnibuses do wear out, that is conceded by all, but omnibus horses and omnibus drivers are by many believed to be immortal. The High Bridge line seems to vindicate this theory, for we imagine we can see hitched to these creaking drags the very same wheezing quadrupeds which struggled up the Yorkville hill, propelled by the identical *whips* who officiated more than thirty years ago. This may be mere surmise, but the resemblance to both is so striking as to give to the theory the full benefit of the doubt. But enough of this wool-gathering.

We left Cato's seated behind the trotter *Ion*. This Ion, named after a favorite character personated by a favorite actress, Miss Ellen Tree, afterward Mrs. Charles Kean, was a good specimen of the road horse of the time; he was a wiry little bay, of the half-broken, pulling type, who could trot *when they had a mind to*, but run away and break things whenever the opportunity offered. He had been trained, like the rest of his class, to walk when on the cobble-stone pavement, and while going at that gait he hung his head to a level with his knees and to all appearance was as gentle as a lamb, but the instant the pavement was passed the brute grabbed the bit, threw out his nose, stiffened his neck, elevated his six inch tail and started on his break-neck dash. In these raids he was usually accompanied by several of his stripe,—we say accompanied, for he was an independent horse he respected neither *whoa* nor *hoa*, and only ceased pulling and dragging when the shed was reached, when, throwing himself back into the breeching, he let go his hold and calmly turned to see if he had succeeded in dislocating the arms of his driver, or rather of the powerless automaton who was being propelled at the will and pleasure of the headstrong brute. Horse trainers have materially changed their views since then, and the theory that arms and reins were better than traces for the promotion of speed is happily exploded.

The Hazard House, located on the crown of

Yorkville Hill at Eighty-second Street, was famous in its day as being the resort of those who delighted in speed and loved to indulge in horse talk. Its extensive stables were filled with animals awaiting purchasers, whose points and merits were intoned with a manner and in language so truthful, so confidential, such language as professional dealers alone are gifted with, that it must be heard to be appreciated, for if attempted by unprofessional pretenders, the charm is at once dispelled. The look, the shrug, the half-unconscious smoothing of a horse's coat, cannot be described; they sell the kicker, the cribber, the lame, the halt, the blind, and with the same unaltered, bland expression congratulate the lucky purchaser,—no, the real professional dealer does not sell, he merely "lets you have,' for in his eyes the noble horse is above price or barter.

The true dealer's love for the horse is to all outward appearance so deeply seated that to part with one, even at his own price, seems to wring the fibres of his tender heart. This love cannot be hypocritical, it must be real; it belongs to this peculiar traffic, and in some special manner is communicated from horse to man; it was apparent at the Hazard House when that famed hostelry was in its prime, it is equally apparent to-day after the lapse of years,—it must be real: Outside barbarians, with no sentiment in their nature, "no music in their souls," do, in their ignorance, rail at these exemplary members of society, call them horse-thieves, and other equally harsh names. Such unbelievers should visit these gentle dealers at their stables, and while inspecting the stock, listen to the soothing tones addressed to each roadster led out for examination; and if still unconverted, take a short drive with the professional horse lover behind some favorite pet, to part with which would be like severing the most tender tie, listen as he chants his praise, and if your heart be not hard as flint it will melt, and the dealer's magic suavity will convict you of unbelief, and force you to confess that you have heretofore wronged a model man. Come, Ion, now for another desperate pull; the last man at the Red House pays the shot.

From Hazard's to the Red House the distance was about one mile, and as the Third Avenue at this point was all down grade, going north, it was a favorite spot for the display of speed. Here on every pleasant afternoon the show of horseflesh was extensive and varied, and did not compare unfavorably with what is seen nowadays on the celebrated Harlem Lane. Rigged to Ford wagons, (Ford was the most noted maker of trotting vehicles of the time,) flyers, double and single, contended for the championship of the *Road*. In memory, on a given day we see George Janeway with Dutchman and mate; Dr. Valk, of Flushing, driving a black team of acknowledged speed; Geo. W. Miller, of the New York Tattersalls, behind Peggy Magie and Ice Pony; William Janeway guiding a pair of cropped sorrels; General Dunham with his powerful Moscow; William Cowan, of the Crosby Street Bazaar, urging Sally Miller; William T. Porter, "The Tall Son of York," shouting vigorously to Confidence in his endeavor to head Abdallah, the famous stallion, handled in those days by Mr. Treadwell, a veteran with the ribbons, who in spurts showed a gait which made the old-fashioned *queue*, which the old gentleman persistently wore until his death, stand out straight behind; while in the crowd were Pelham, Honest John, Cayuga Maid, Lady Bemis, Tacony, Mac, and scores of other *good ones*, all striving for the lead at the Red House Gate. It was on this speeding ground that the world-renowned Flora Temple made her first appearance. For a time this cross-grained, wiry, and occasionally sulky little bay mare was owned and driven by John C. Perrin. She had been brought to New York to sell by a Washington Hollow dealer, who in his turn had selected her from a drove at the low figure of eighty dollars. Though she had no known pedigree, her fine blood-like head, well-set neck, firm shoulders, straight back, powerful forearms and general display of muscle, attracted the attention of the shrewd horseman. After more than ordinary care and training at the hands of her owner, she gradually developed the qualities of a first-class trotter,—the crazy flights, half-racking, half-trotting little bay mare settled down into a true stepper. She was at once put upon the track, and though successful in the main, her wonderful powers developed slowly. One of her subsequent drivers, James D. McMann, has always claimed that he was certain that some day she would prove a wonder. But Mr. Perrin and his friends little dreamed of the triumph she would achieve in her prime. She became the favorite wonder of the sporting world,—such a wonder, that owners of certain strains of blood and breeders of certain localities hotly contended for the credit which would attach to her birthplace. After many hotly contested races against the most noted flyers the country could produce, she had emblazoned on her stall, "*Flora Temple, Queen of the Trotting Turf*—2.19 3-4." As but few competitors ventured to dispute her title, the wonderful animal was devoted by her owners to the somewhat doubtful performances at agricultural fairs; and, accompanied by the celebrated Ethan Allen and Princess, the tour of the United States was made. Everywhere, at fairs and on race tracks, the Queen was greeted with cheers. She still lives, crowned with years, though within a short time her brilliant record has been wiped out by Dexter, Goldsmith Maid and one or two more celebrities on the turf.

About the same date another horse celebrity appeared, and attracted much attention both on the road and track. A long-bodied, low-swinging grey mare was now and then driven over from Long Island, and challenged all for a friendly brush on the avenue. Lady Suffolk, the animal referred to, had made her debut on the Beacon Track, a race-course located a few miles back of Hoboken, and extensively patronized by the horsemen of New York. On her first appearance, both the man and her driver demonstrated that neither were unsophisticated. She was entered in a *green* purse, and won so handily that some tall *talking* was indulged in by the owners and drivers of her discomfited competitors. Dave Bryant, the owner and driver of Lady Suffolk, knew the wonderful powers of his mare, but he was penurious and egotistical in the extreme. He overworked and maltreated the noble creature while she, in spite of all drawbacks, developed speed and lasting qualities which for years were unequalled ; and there are not a few trainers of the present day who affirm that, had Suffolk been handled with the care now exercised, her performances would to-day have stood unrivalled on the trotting turf. Others might be noticed, but these bright *horse stars* will suffice to show that the *tabooed* Third Avenue was not destitute of attractions for the lover of the noble horse, and that the reader may be enabled to inspect at leisure and comment on them and their drivers let him lounge for an hour or so on the broad piazza of the Red House.

The Red House was located on a plot of many acres, which was entered from Third Avenue by a road at about the point where One Hundred and Fifth Street is now cut through to the Harlem River. The main building was originally the residence of William McGowan, whose descendants are still the possessors of an extended domain in the immediate vicinity. It was a roomy edifice, admirably adapted for a public road house, while the extensive grounds, upon which there was a well-kept, half-mile trotting course, offered extraordinary inducements to the drivers, and consequently made it a prominent resort. One of its earliest proprietors was Lewis Rogers. He was a dapper little man, always dressed in the tip of fashion and as neat and trim in the appointments of his house, as in his personal attire. Fancy dogs, rare singing birds, choice plants were his special weakness, while the walls of his rooms were covered with the most tasteful engravings money could purchase. Like a wise publican, he spared neither time nor means in stocking both his cellar and larder with the choicest commodities in the market. In this last he was doubtless aided and encouraged by his father-in-law, for what old or middle-aged resident does not with pleasure recall the good cheer dispensed by Edmund Jones, first at the Second Ward Hotel, in Nassau Street between Fulton and John, and subsequently, until his death, at the celebrated Claremont, on the Bloomingdale Road. After years of life and passing associations have almost imperceptibly crowded one and another from memory, the ideal of Lew Rogers remains as vivid as when daily seen and conversed with in youth. He was a "*big*" little man—not only a courteous host, but a host in himself. He was an accomplished horseman, thoroughly versed in the mysterious lingo of the craft, and always posted up in the secrets of the knowing ones. We youngsters listened to him as to an oracle, and received his opinions on such vital points as were mooted, without question or doubt. He was *posted* in the varied sporting intelligence of the period; obtained by his winning manner to all grades who patronized his house—in fine, we looked upon him as a walking encyclopædia of horse racing, cock fighting, rat baiting, prize fighting, and the other *innocent* pastimes in which we clandestinely indulged, against the advice and consent of our respected sires and guardians.

The Red House was just the spot to lounge away an hour; it afforded ample scope for the study of character, as each class of citizens was sure to be represented. The Broadway exquisite was there in the person of "Dandy Marx." This conspicuous and eccentric young man was tall and slight, by no means ill favoed, and possessed far more brains than he was credited with by the community at large. He dressed in the English *negligé* style, then considered *outré*, but which at present would be far behind the mode, besides he wore a moustache, at the time looked upon as a foreign assumption—in fact he dressed and demeaned himself in advance of his time. Born at the South, he usually spoke with the drawl of a genuine cockney, and assumed in public the stiff, reticent air of a London *nob*. His equipages were many and varied, copied from foreign models, and he dressed his servants in livery which was a marked peculiarity as compared with Knickerbocker simplicity. He usually rode unaccompanied in his dray, driving a splendid team, and not unfrequently sported a four-in-hand which he handled with consummate skill. Marx was truly a prominent character; he did not mingle in ladies' society, though his mother and sisters were always attired in the height of fashion, and were possessed of an ample fortune. There was a seclusiveness about the family circle which was ever unexplained. As a rule Marx was alone in his strolls or drives, the exception being the presence of his sister, who was acknowledged to be a horsewoman of rare excellence.

In the person of William Harrington we had

before us a representative man of a very different but numerous class. He was the famous leader of a type now rapidly becoming extinct, and which in his and their time were styled *Bowery Boys*. These Boys were, to say the least, peculiar, in their habits, demeanor and conversation; but they must not on that score be confounded or identified with the rough outlaws of to-day who pretend to legitimate succession; for even though the latter spring from the same source, it is not true. The B'hoy of thirty years since did not associate with imported criminals; there was a pride in his peculiar swagger which his modern imitators vainly attempt. The Bowery Boy of old did not live upon plunder or his wits, he was early apprenticed to some trade; to be a "boss butcher" was the acme of his ambition. His week days were spent in performing the labor of his peculiar calling, which was only suspended for the time when the alarm of fire impelled him to drop his implements of trade and rush to meet his engine on her headlong way to aid in extinguishing a conflagration. On Sunday or special holidays the B'hoy appeared a different man. His sleek beaver, his well-greased locks carefully rolled over each cheek, while at the back of his round head the hair was clipped as short as scissors could cut; closely-shaven face, for he affected to despise the effeminacy of a beard; black pants fitting tightly to the knee, from which point they gradually increased in width until when the foot was reached it was almost hidden by the expanse of broad-cloth; tight-fitting black frock coat with skirts of formidable length, a gaily-flowered silk waistcoat with ample shirt collar of spotless white about completed his gala attire. When thus arrayed it was a treat indeed to see him sauntering along, accompanied by his fancifully bedecked gal, and his favorite bull terrier, the lord of the Bowery. Of this class William Harrington was an acknowledged leader. He was a man of large frame and wonderful strength. For years he figured in the "roped arena," and not a few powerful opponents were compelled to own him master. Boss Harrington, as he was familiarly styled, was an actor in all the excitements of his time, whether at the polls during election, for he was an uncompromising Whig; or on the race-course when Boston and Fashion were straining every muscle for victory, he was prominent in the foreground, a protector to the weak and timid, a terror to sneak-thieves and ruffians. A butcher by trade, he amassed an ample competency which in after-life he scattered in companionship with his admirers with a too lavish hand, and ended his career of excitement and sport by passing away when full of years, either by suicide as some aver, or by the hand of some cowardly assassin. Another *genus homo* was always to be met with at the Red House, and a brief description of one or two of the most marked specimens will suffice to convey a correct idea of the fraternity. Sam Segue was a well-known horse dealer; his home, if memory correctly serves, was at Albany, but New York was the usual field he preferred for the display of his equine blandishments. The stock he dealt in was, as a rule, first-class, and in most instances he confined his attention to carriage teams. Style, not speed, was his forte. Sam was a rubicund man, with a well-cultivated bland expression of the eye, and so far as the public knew, a model of amiability. His anxiety seemed to lay in what exact proportion he should divide his superabundant love between horse and customer. The "pictures" he had to dispose of were his special care; they were groomed to a nicety, and each particular hair in mane or tail so arranged as to do its whole duty. He carefully studied all the minute appointments of his turnout, and in trim neatness he was far ahead of his few competitors in the market. Broadway in the morning and the road in the afternoon were his parade grounds, where, with a single eye to business, he carelessly nodded to some passing acquaintance, though he never forgot the main issue in bringing prominently to view the telling points of the "star-gazers" he was then guiding with a master hand. Ever on the alert to check on the instant any impropriety the unruly beasts might attempt, and at the same time assume an easy confident manner which would convince all passers-by of the perfect training and docility of his team. Well oiled, well peppered, well checked up, they were no slouches, and to use one of Sam's well remembered favorite expressions, "they were no mud-turtles, but fixed their gaze on the attic windows as they trotted past." Sam was a sharp dealer in a trade "when Greek met Greek," and had the credit of being seldom over-reached. As a talker he was awarded the first premium at Tattersalls, then prominently located on Broadway, between Grand and Howard, and whether he is still chanting equine praises, or has abandoned his original field of usefulness, the writer is ignorant; certain it is that for long years his genial face has been missed, and no one of the present generation of professional horsemen resembles in the faintest degree the remembrance of Sam Segue, the king of jockeys. Rowan was a confrère and cotemporary with Segue. Though he was actively engaged in the same delectable calling, the men were perfect antipodes of each other. Rowan was called Mr. Rowan. If he possessed any Christian name it was never mentioned outside of the sacred precinct of his domestic circle, for there was a something in his appearance which acted as a bar to the slightest approach to familiarity. In dress and address he assumed the clerical style. A suit of sombre black, generally well glazed with continuous wear, constituted his outside gear, and he invariably donned a white cravat to make the imitation more perfect. His manner was in keeping with his apparel; cold, smileless, reticent, he relied upon his peculiar make-up to proclaim his pretensions to extra honesty. Could such a saintly being conceal a fault or hide a blemish? Irresponsible stable boys, doubtless actuated by malice, did venture to assert that this pattern man at times employed his tongue in the use of other words than those especially adapted for prayers, and that he would furiously belabor some poor beast which had unwittingly winced or wheezed, and by such unseemly conduct had broken up a prosperous trade, but in public he was never seen to maltreat a horse or heard to utter an oath during the long years of his industry, which was proverbial and knew no bounds. Six days of the week he devoted to the buying, selling and trading of cripples of every grade, and on the seventh day arrayed in a fresh white cravat and a more presentable suit of sable, he dedicated himself to exhorting sinners to repentance at a Methodist church where he figured as a prominent pillar and a shining light. With such an example on record who will dare assert that passionate love for the horse is incompatible with the exercise of high moral qualities in man. Many, doubtless, who still linger in Gotham can readily recall the man described. They will bear witness that if Rowan was tricky he never betrayed any outward evidence of success, and that the pocket in which he carried his money, if he ever possessed any of the filthy lucre, was always under strong lock and key; his charities must have been unostentatious, if charity was one of the attributes of his humanity. A character, he existed long in our midst. The above will suffice as the extremes of a class far less numerous then than now; the trade has changed with the increased demand. Railroad and omnibus companies require vast numbers of horses then rarely dealt in, and the men now prominent at Bull's Head should more properly be styled contractors, for the wholesale traffic has divested them of the peculiarities of the old-time jockey, whose sympathies were engrossed in one quadruped, or at most a pair, and on it or them he lavished the concentrated enthusiasm incident to his peculiar calling.

Passing to another and very different type of

visitors who frequented the Red House, a man is recalled who for the quarter of a century stood prominent and alone in his adopted vocation. William T. Porter, the founder and editor of *The Spirit of the Times*, a journal which was for years the acknowledged organ of the sports of turf and field. "The tall Son of York," as he was familiarly styled by his many friends throughout the length and breadth of the land, combined in his person all the requisite qualities to ensure success. His presence was comanding, of extraordinary height, with perfect proportion of limb; a finely formed head, and a countenance which gave unmistakable assurance of intellect, culture and refinement of the highest order. Endowed by nature with warm and tender sympathies, he drew around him by his peculiar magnetism the most accomplished writers of the day, among whom the late William Henry Herbert figured conspicuously, and whose works on the horse are still the standard text books of the breeders of America. Manly, invigorating sport was the topic of the *Spirit*, and it pervaded Porter's sanctum in Barclay Street. Blooded stock was his darling hobby, and woe betide the luckless wight who could not produce a clear and well authenticated pedigree for his entry. By untiring industry and clear application Porter's mind became a storehouse of equine lore; he became the umpire in all disputed points, and his marvelous memory was the wonder of turfmen north, south, east and west. Every true sportsman became his ally and contributed to the success of his paper; so for a time he was on the high road to fame and fortune. Lavishly liberal, his purse was always open to succor the needy, and as a consequence scores of idle, worthless toadies became the recipients of his generous but indiscriminate bounty. Such was Porter in his early prime. Courted, caressed, flattered, his walk among kindred spirits was always an ovation. Guileless as a little child he bestowed no thought on the morrow; full of animal life, with good will toward all, his leisure moments were devoted to pleasure and the companionship of wits who ministered to his weaknesses, and he enjoyed the passing hour to the "top of his bent." Neglecting his golden opportunity to amass riches, the world in its ceaseless roll passed him by with the refuse of the age, and he woke as from a dream to find himself broken, friendless and alone. He had followed his much-loved brothers, Olcott, George and Frank, all known men of rare talent, to their last resting place, and the flatterers who had basked in the noontide of his prosperity deserted him as the evening shadows of poverty drew nigh. To the disappointed, broken-hearted man no solace presented itself save the draught which blunts the recollection of ingratitude and soothes the pangs engendered by wasted opportunities. To that fatal draught he fled and clung to it until with shattered mind and wasted frame he was mercifully called to his long *home*.

For professional drivers and trainers the Red House was a favorite rendezvous. To them the race track was the main attraction, for rarely a day passed when their services were not required for some impromptu match. Charley Brooks,

Jake Somenidyke, Isaac Woodruff, George Spicer, Clark Vandewater, James D. McMann, etc., were usually on hand, while occasionally Hiram Woodruff, William Wheeler, and Sim Hoagland would put in an appearance and give us outsiders a sight at some noted flyers who could "knock spots" out of three minutes. Americus, Trustee (trotted twenty miles within the hour), Ned Forrest, Yankee Doodle, Confidence, Rattler, Whalebone, Pelham, with lots of private nags, whose names are now forgotten because their deeds were unsung, would frequently give us a touch of their quality which would end with the usual amount of "horse talk," and "drinks all round" at the expense of the unfortunate owner of the animal which for that special day chanced to be "out of fix." What "out of fix" rightly means no one ever rightly understands, but it is always assigned as the reason for every defeat ever met with on the turf. Horsemen never have and never will cry "beaten;" their motto is "try, try again," and in that spirit lies the life of sport.

Many are the amusing anecdotes recalled by the associations connected with the Red House, but unfortunately some of the prominent actors are still around, and lively at that; and these might possibly think the recital of their youthful frolics and indiscretions would detract somewhat from their present dignified positions as respected grandsires, and members in high standing with our best metropolitan society. So we are compelled to desist as most of the incidents would be pointless if stripped of personality.

But before bidding farewell to a spot fraught

with so many pleasing reminiscences, we cannot forbear recording a passing tribute to a man who was for years its lessee, and during whose tenure the time-honored hostelry retained its prestige undimmed ; but on whose departure for more central and accessible quarters, it became in truth "a banquet hall deserted." Its course was run, and the old structure now untenanted shows no vestige of its former attractions to arrest the attention of the present generation. Ned Luff was for many years one of the most obliging, generous and popular hosts on the road. He was eminently a progressive man, and in that lay the prime secret of his success. He lived up to the requirements of the times, kept young, and so adapted his house and its surroundings to meet the special demands of each succeeding class of patrons. He argued tastes change, for he had seen over and over again one set of riders tire of the care and expense which invariably accompany the ownership of fast horses, sell out to another set anxious to try its luck in the mysteries and mazes of horsedom, the last soon disappearing from the drive, but being followed by another, surely "as the night the day." Many of these changes occurred during the term in which Luff dispensed creature comforts; but each new flock of pleasure-seekers seemed by intuition to find him out, and no old roadster would pass his door without making a desperate lunge for the shed. To all he was courteous and acceptable, ending his career a publican in the harness of his trade on Harlem Lane. Jolly, free-hearted, he had hosts of friends, and no enemy, save one, who overruled his better judgment and hurried him to an untimely grave. Poor Luff; the word "No" had not been taught him in youth; he could not utter it even to King Alcohol. Goodbye to the Red House, too many painful thoughts of passing away present themselves; let us seek other sights which may be found at Bradshaw's, at Harlem.

About one mile north of the Red House, on a fine, level road over Harlem Flats, was situated Bradshaw's Hotel. The curious in such matters can at any time inspect all that remains of the once famous hostelry by halting for a moment on the corner of Third Avenue and One Hundred and Twenty-fifth Street. The roomy, double frame building is still there, but the grade having been materially changed, the old piazza which in former days afforded ample breathing and lounging room for the guests has been torn away, the former parlor converted into a drug store, the wide hall is used for the sale of segars, newspapers and soda water, by the famous ball player, Thompson, and the old bar-room occupied as a bakery. "Here she goes and there she goes"—thousands will recall the threadbare anecdote of former times—seems to be written all over the venerable pile, and Thompson will point out to anyone the exact spot where the old clock stood. That the visitors at Bradshaw's were many, it is only necessary to state that the extensive sheds on the north and west were insufficient to accommodate the quadrupeds, and the additional one erected on the opposite side of the avenue was often crowded. Bradshaw's being but a few hundred yards from Harlem Bridge was virtually the turning point of the drive, and consequently a long rest was taken by many who made it their only stopping place on the road.

There were at that time moderate as well as fast men, and though both classes of riders patronized this unexceptionable house we will more particularly notice some of those who did not habitually pull up either at the Red House or Hazard's. Besides this class of our own citizens there were quite a number of the residents of Westchester, Pelham, New Rochelle, etc., who were frequent visitors on the drive, that they might "air a green colt," and take some of the conceit out of the Gothamites by giving the dust to some favorite roadster. Of New Yorkers who were *habitues*, we recall William Vyse, a gentleman who for many seasons drove a bay horse, which for size, speed and action combined would challenge competition to-day among the thousands of splendid, high-bred animals to be seen in Central Park, horses which are the pride of the breeders of Orange County and Kentucky. He was as large and heavy-limbed as a truck horse, his coat was as silky as a thoroughbred, and at every point exhibited indisputable signs of blood. His action was high and nimble, and there were few animals on the road that could beat him to the pavements, rigged as he generally was to a heavy two-wheeled tilbury, and his owner, who was sociable in his disposition, was rarely unaccompanied by a boon companion.

Next on the list, and always a welcome arrival, was the genial George L. Pride, a great admirer of fine horses. Gentleman George affected style rather than speed, and his turnout was always in perfect keeping with the outward appearance of the man; neat, trim, expensive, but never gaudy. Under all circumstances both driver and horse were invariably cool and self-possessed, ever ready for effect. No fatigue was ever indicated by either, and a most perfect understanding seemed to exist between master and servant as the stately grey ambled slowly up the road. George Pride was a singular compound; a sort of providential blessing in his way, for he formed the exciting topic at many a tea party, which otherwise would have proved a silent, unseasoned meeting. In his day New York could produce but few young men, or middle-aged men, who were not actively engaged in business pursuits, consequently Broadway, from Canal Street to the Battery, (the only promenade), was given over almost entirely to the belles and their mammas for uninterrupted shopping, which was then a much more serious occupation than the gala pastime it now presents. But few male interlopers intruded upon the fair damsels to distract them during the momentuous duty of selecting the same pattern of the same stuff which everybody else wore, but prominent among the few was Pride, who always sauntered along dressed in his most precise style. His manner toward the fair sex was invariably respectful and undemonstrative, at times even bashful as a timid girl; still there was a certain something about the man which would attract the ladies, and render him always a choice morsel of gossip with spinsters and dames. Old men did not exactly know whence came the abundant means which enabled him to lead an apparently idle life; the old maids looked doubtfully over their spectacles, while the young girls could not help casting sly, furtive glances at the good-looking mystery they almost invariably met in their morning strolls. Thus for many long years George lived and thrived, and was conspicuous until lost in the rapid growth of the city, which growth has proved a death-blow to all individuality in our midst. Were he alive to-day he could pass unknown and unnoticed from Harlem River to the Battery, save by the few who claimed kindred or courted some favor. Such the difference between the Knickerbocker city and the metropolis of New York.

Up drive a bevy of young men who were called gay in those days, who lived at a fashionable boarding-house, presided over by Miss Margaret Mann, a famous woman then, and she would be now in this bloomer age. Her house was a small hotel, and the stopping place of noted travelers who visited the city. It was located at No. 61 Broadway, just below and in close proximity to Wall Street. From its front windows could be daily seen fashion, beauty and wealth, wending their way to and from the shady walks of the Battery. In those days to hail from Miss Mann's was a sure passport, and the young men who could afford the luxury, (one dollar per day), were sure to be known to fame. Some of them kept their horses, and good ones at that, at Henry Walters' stable on Lumber Street. A most miserable shed it would appear if compared with the palatial equine bazaars now so common in our midst. After the toil of the day was over they would spin up to Bradshaw's. Of these *bloods*, Ned Andareise, Frank Waldo, Wash McLean,—the Colonel still lives a splendid monument of early piety and outdoor exercise,—Dick Sheppard, Frank Stevenson, and one or two more who afterwards fell from grace, viz.; became poor, were fair specimens of the respectable fashionable class. Precise in their dress and appointments, they were careful not to violate openly any of the prescribed conventionalities of life. They wore gay, not dissipated, for dissipation was ranked with low vulgarity, and was a certain bar to success. By the crowd on the road and by men who were their equals in everything but self-control, they were pronounced proud upstarts; yet, notwithstanding all this prudence, the love of the horse and of sport was in them, and before the magic theme of horse talk they threw aside all conventional reserve and listened with eagerness to the orator of the day.

A frequent horse orator at Bradshaw's, was a well-known Westchester man, who would have proved a rare subject for the pen of Boz, as in richness of surroundings he far surpassed the obese parent of Mr. Samuel Weller. Gilley Browne cannot be fitly described. Were he still in the land of the living, the presidency of the fat men's association would be conceded to him beyond a doubt. He was a ponderous individual, and as jolly as he was weighty. Rich, far beyond his necessities, by inheritance, he naturally took to horses, and became in his own peculiar way a most inveterate trader in stock, and to that he devoted the entire time he could spare from his prime duty to himself, viz., eating and drinking. That Gilley was sometimes "stuck" in a "swap" is not singular ; but his uniform good nature when he ascertained the fact made him a perfect hero in our juvenile eyes. Beset by sharps on every side, he managed somehow to get rid of his hard bargains without omitting a meal or denying himself a single drink. Rumor had it that when he chanced upon "something very bad" he headed at once for New Rochelle, for the purpose of having a trade with a man who never failed him in his extremity; for Bill Shute could manage the sale of anything that stood on "all fours," and in case Gilley was successful, would kindly lend him a "kicker" to reach home. Gilley's visits to Shute were not unfrequent, and were looked upon as gala days by the bar-room loungers. Both men were sharp, treats were frequent, and old Falstaff whether ahead in pocket or "dead broke," always left for home in the " wee small hours" as happy as a lord. This was the Gilley Brown who was always honored by a large audience as he wheezingly discoursed on the superlative merits of some favorite roadster, which was invariably pronounced as entirely too valuable "to cart him around." Bruce Hunter, Tom Reynolds, Sam Cowdrey, Den McCreedy, and other Westchester riders always welcomed the fat man as a genuine companion on the road. We regret quitting Bradshaw's and its many past associations so abruptly, but time warns us, so we will jog back to the city by the Bloomingdale Road, bid adieu to speed, horse talk and trotting dust, while taking a retrospective glance at the more quiet resorts, frequented by those who did not consider the Third Avenue and its bustle quite *comme il faut.*

What is now One Hundred and Twenty-Fifth Street was the traveled road which crossed the northern end of the Island. It intersected the Bloomingdale Road at the foot of the hill, where the suburb of Manhattanville, now grown to respectable dimensions, is located. Above this point of intersection there were but few residences of any special pretensions, and not a single hotel until Kingsbridge was reached. The mansion of Madame Jumel, famous as the widow of Aaron Burr, was perhaps the most extensive and imposing; the Bradhurst estate, on the corner of Breakneck Hill, now being leveled and "citified" by the serpentine St. Nicholas Avenue, which has swallowed up Harlem Lane, name and all, was next in prominence, while the more unpretentious houses of Shepherd Knapp, Gideon Lee and Richard F. Carman are the only residences of any note recalled. Carmansville and the sumptuous homes of Washington Heights have sprung up like magic, and the coming generation will witness improvements in that once rocky locality which will be unequalled in any city in the world. South of One Hundred and Twenty-Fifth Street the Bloomingdale Road was far more thickly settled. On the Hudson River, at this point, still stands a venerable pile, now and for many years past known as Claremont. This elegant structure was originally reared for a private residence. The spacious building bears witness to the enlarged ideas and ample means of the projector, while his taste in selection of locality is amply testified by the grand view which is afforded from every point. Its rear overlooks the noble Hudson, and the *coup d'oeil* on a clear day, reaches from the Highlands of Neversink to St. Anthony's Nose and the Palisades, its equal for extent and beauty rarely met with during extended travel. Thousands have enjoyed the enchanting scene since the house became a public resort, and was made famous as a house of entertainment many years since by the late Edmund Jones.

This Bloomingdale Road has now virtually passed away. Seemingly only a short time since it was a country drive of unsurpassed beauty, "up hill and down dale," varied with many a curve, and at short intervals enlivened by an enchanting view of the noble Hudson. Independent of its numerous public resorts, many unpretending country seats were scattered along, whose occupants, mostly of Knickerbocker origin, little dreamed in their quiet seclusion how soon their favorite landmarks and bowers were to be swept away by the greed of public improvement. The Abbey and Woodlawn, both situated south of Claremont, were largely patronized in their day. The latter, once the residence of Dr. Moffatt, the original "pill man" of America, was very popular under the management of Capt. W. L. Wiley, who is still a resident of the district, and a great political favorite in his immediate neighborhood. Next, jogging down a steep lane, we alight at a secluded little snuggery called Stryker's Bay, one of the most unpretending yet attractive houses on the drive. At that time its landlord was a

Mr. Francis, who during his proprietorship perfected his celebrated life-boat, which invention subsequently made him both famous and rich. The little house was in a nook sheltered from all points, save from the west, where the fine view of the Hudson amply repaid many a visitor.

Adjoining Stryker's Bay on the south, and separated only by a minute inlet was the Summer retreat of Dr. Valentine Mott. It presented no special attractions of interest for the curious, but seemed to have been selected by its owner simply as a quiet resting place, where real relaxation from the toils and cares of an arduous professional career could be had without restraint or the fear of interruption.

In close proximity to the last mentioned place, and the point where Ninety-second Street, formerly known as Jauncy Lane, intersects the Grand Boulevard, was located the elegant and expensive country seat of Colonel Thorne, one of the most dashing men of his generation. His fine physique and courtly bearing was proverbial. During many years of his fashionable career he resided permanently at Paris and was one of the prominent notables of that gay metropolis during the reign of Louis Phillippe. In early life Col. Thorne married Miss Jauncy, a wealthy heiress, whose family ranked high among the Knickerbockers. This pretentious home was situated in an enclosure of many acres, thickly studded with towering elms of great beauty. Many of the trees still stand ; the more elaborate, highly-furnished house is fast going to decay, and the name of Elm Park, the scene of many costly and aristocratic entertainments, is now only associated with lager bier, target excursions and cheap summer balls.

Burnham's Mansion House. Thousands of middle-aged men and women can to-day recall the many gambols they enjoyed in childhood on Burnham's lawn; they cannot fail remembering with vividness the smile of welcome they received from the kind old host and his motherly wife, who were always at the door "to welcome the coming, speed the parting guest." The girls will not have forgotten the large square parlor where the cake and lemonade were dispensed after their hearty run to and from the summer house on the bank, or their protracted stroll through that old-fashioned garden, with its box borders and its profusion of gay native flowers. The boys never will forget, "while memory lasts," George, Jim and William, three as devoted sons and delightful hosts as ever can be met; modest, spirited, well-trained American boys, who could gracefully acknowledge a kindness, and with true dignity resent an insult. Burnham's was fitly styled the family house of the drive. On each fine Summer afternoon the spacious grounds were filled with ladies and children, who sauntered at their leisure, having no fear of annoyance and confident of perfect immunity from insult. The honest, high-toned reputation of the host and his family acted as a most efficient police, and was indeed a terror to the evil disposed. The large family circle, save one daughter, have all paid the debt to nature. James C., "Jim," as he was familiarly and widely known, was the latest survival. After an honorable career as commandant of the New York Volunteers in the Mexican War, he was taken off while yet a young man by disease contracted in that arduous campaign, thus closing honorably the career of that much respected family. With the death of James the reputation of the old stopping place vanished, and though for several subsequent years its doors remained open as if to invite the passers-by to enter, its prestige was gone, its glory had departed, and it became a thing of the past.

One moment with Corporal Thompson and the drive on Manhattan Island is ended. Where the Fifth Avenue Hotel now stands, with its highly-wrought marble front and richly draped plate glass windows, was the site of a diminutive frame structure, surrounded by what might be termed "a five acre lot," which was used, when used at all, for cattle exhibitions. This was the hostelry of Corporal Thompson, the last stopping place for codgers, old and young. Laverty, Winans, Niblo, the Costers, Hones, Whitneys, Schermerhorns, the genial Sol Kipp, Doctor Vaché, Ogden Hoffman, Nat Blunt, and scores more of *bon vivants*, hail fellows well met, would here end their ride for the day by "smiling" with the worthy Corporal, and wash down any of their former improprieties with a sip of his *ne plus ultra*, which was always kept in reserve for a special nightcap. There was a special magnetism about the snug little bar-room, always trim as a lady's boudoir, which induced the desire to tarry awhile, as if that visit were destined to be the last, so it frequently happened that a jolly party was compelled to grope slowly homewards through the unlighted gloomy road which led to the city.

Good-bye to the Bloomingdale Road! Adieu to the once famous Third Avenue! for both are gone forever. The former has been swallowed by the aristocratic conventional Boulevard, which is rapidly filling its valleys, levelling its hillocks and straightening its once graceful curves, while the latter long since succumbed to the grasping power of a railroad which has driven sport away to make room for traffic and gain.

Any old resident who may by chance cast his eye over these cursory and imperfect recollections, will find ample food for reflection, by spending a quiet half hour at the Fifth Avenue entrance of the Central Park. Even that brief time will suffice to convince him that he is *but a pilgrim and a stranger* in the city where he was born. No matter how well-known he may be in a circle which he considers extensive and perhaps influential, he will discover that he is an atom of small import, unnoticed by the throng, occupying the costly equipages which enters the drive in one continuous trail. Any attempt, to scan in detail the imposing procession, he will soon find an impossibility. A general idea of lavish expenditure, of reckless dash will possess his mind; the longer his eye is fixed upon the richly caparisoned, prancing steeds, the endless variety of splendid carriages, the fanciful and at times grotesque costumes of the occupants, the greater will be his bewilderment. Queries will flash through his brain. Who are all these people? Whence do they come? What is the source of this boundless wealth? The answer can only be had by retrospection and reflection. On looking back he will remember where he is standing, and will remember when he was born, a half century since Park Place was *well up town* with only a scattering population beyond.

He will then see what untold millions are now represented by the costly architectural piles which now stand between the Central Park and the rear of that old City Hall which was inexpensively finished by our prudent forefathers, for the reason that it would never be seen; he will in his mind's eye glance over and calculate the value of the acres of warehouses lying between these points, filled to overflowing with the costliest fabrics that the looms of the civilized world can produce; he will note the number of spacious hotels, whose inmates alone would nearly equal the population of the city at the date of his nativity. Let him go farther and contrast the lightning speed of the locomotive with the old rumbling stage, the ocean steamer with the dull packet, the telegraph with the slow mail wagon. Let him recall the marvellous strides in the mechanical arts, and realize that minutes now can accomplish that which consumed laborious hours when he was young. Such retrospection will enable any one who has slept in a humdrum existence, while the world moved on, to realize the source of the marvellous wealth which *is* so rapidly beautifying cosmopolitan New York

CONCLUSION.

Knickerbocker life in New York is among the things that were. Suddenly accumulated wealth has swept away its commemorative monuments. Boulevards and avenues have swallowed its winding streets; the leveling spirit of progress has smoothed the hillocks that were hindrances to the speed of this flashing era. Imposing structures of marble and granite have "in the twinkling of an eye" displaced modest piles of homely brick, and costly luxuries driven simple necessities to the wall. The comparison of the brilliant gas light to the glimmering taper fails to define the marvellous transition.

From the cemetery of past recollections the old Knickerbocker home, like Banquo's ghost, seems "to burst its cerements." With mournful gaze, the well-remembered power of a recent past, grieves that it has so soon been forgotten, when but a few years since its title to respect was undisputed; its mandates obeyed by old and young, rich and poor. In fancy the towering giant of the past stands erect as of yore, commanding in its authoritative mien. Its unflinching eye, lighted up with the consciousness of assured rectitude, is rivited upon the gay, restless throng flitting from flower to flower with excited glee, chasing one after another the senseless frivolities with which Fashion has strewn the highways and byways of modernized Gotham. Its lips appear to move, and a faint "Well! well!" falls upon the ear. This old-time cry was of great import to Knickerbocker youth; it was sure to be heard when some express "fireside" injunction had been disregarded, or some act of wilful disobedience detected. Such of grandmother's children as may still be alive can attest the weighty significance that attached to the tiny monosyllable, for they cannot fail to recall her calm deliberation of utterance, the expression of hopeless doubt which at the time clouded her placid face, the searching glance peering above her spectacles, the slow swaying to and fro of her venerable form, stayed only when a deep-drawn sigh had brought relief to her wounded heart. The "Well! well!" was grandmother's text; the beginning, the ending of her lecture; it was typical of her despair. After it had been solemnly given out, the meeting between judge and culprit was a silent protrac'ed session. During this trying ordeal the kind old lady was sustained by her undying faith in the efficacy of the Fifth Commandment, but as soon as the first evidence of penitential sorrow was manifested by the erring child, her bright, smiling forgiveness dried the tears of contrition, and promises "rich and rare" were showered upon the broken spirit,—wounded only to bless.

This "Well! well!" of forty years ago is a most fitting lament as the fact stares us in the face that ruling Fashion has decreed "home, sweet home" shall be no more. The mandate affects alike the arrogant denizen of the mansion and the humble inmate of the cabin. Palace, mansion, residence, tenement, become henceforth only conventional names by which man's places of shelter are known, and merely express degrees regulated by capital, but all despoiled of their magnetic attraction.

Cold prose is utterly inadequate to convey the refined sentiment clustering about and around the Knickerbocker home. The much admired poet whose familiar strain commences with "The birds singing gaily that came at my call," is compelled to own the grand theme beyond his scope, and admit by comparison, "There is no place like home." But deeper than the most subtle vein of poetry can delve, far down in the hidden recesses of man's soul where its tendrils are imbedded, it is a felt but indescribable reality,—a living need. This Knickerbocker home was the theatre of woman's legitimate duties; the stage upon which her accomplishments shone with most refulgent lustre; the realm of mother, sister, wife. It was the elysium of childhood; the cradle in which petty cares were rocked to sleep with soothing lullabies that never fade; the play-ground where tottering steps were tenderly guarded by outstretched arms. It was the nursery of mind, affection, character, the "Alma Mater" to which the weary, the weak, the dispirited fled for rest as to an enchanted shrine fanned by the soft wing of gentle Peace. Its code was founded on love, based on family honor; it framed the laws to which society obsequiously bowed.

[THE END.]

www.ingramcontent.com/pod-product-compliance
Lightning Source LLC
Chambersburg PA
CBHW031944230426
43672CB00010B/2044